THE AMERICA WE DESERVE

OTHER BOOKS BY DONALD J. TRUMP

The Art of the Deal

Surviving at the Top

The Art of the Comeback

THE AMERICA
WE DESERVE

DONALD J. TRUMP

WITH DAVE SHIFLETT

RENAISSANCE BOOKS
Los Angeles

Also available from Audio Renaissance:

The America We Deserve
Read by the author • Abridged
ISBN: 1-55927-579-0 • $19.95

Library of Congress Catalog Card Number: 99-068932
ISBN: 1-58063-131-2

10 9 8 7 6 5 4 3 2 1

Design by Jesus Arellano

Published by Renaissance Books
Distributed by St. Martin's Press
Manufactured in the United States of America
First Edition

To Fred and Mary Trump,
who believed so deeply in the American dream

ACKNOWLEDGMENTS

To my able right arm, Norma Foerderer who read and reread the manuscript to perfection.

To my friend and associate the tough and tireless Roger Stone who has done so much to oversee its production.

To the people at Renaissance Books for their energy and support: Bill Hartley, my insightful publisher; Arthur Morey, my resourceful editor; Ann Hartley, my tireless copy editor; and to the staff of the company.

To Nick Ribis—no one works harder.

And to Jesse Ventura, whose breakthrough in Minnesota caused me to start thinking about the role people outside government must play to help our country.

CONTENTS

★   ★   ★

The Serious Side of Trump

L ET'S CUT TO THE CHASE. Yes, I am considering a run for the presidency of the United States. The reason has nothing to do with vanity, as some have suggested, or merely to block the advancement of other candidates. I will run if I become convinced I can win. Two things are certain at this point, however: I believe nonpoliticians represent the wave of the future and if elected I would make the kind of president America needs in the new millennium.

You can see a long way from the top of Trump Tower. If you stand here beside me and look one direction, the view is outstanding. Economic growth is hitting 6 percent. New York is the hottest city on the planet—hotter than Hong Kong and hotter than Shanghai, which had a crane on every corner in the early 1990s. Our crime rate is way down, thanks to Rudy Giuliani, our great mayor. I'm having more fun than I've ever had. In this terrific economic climate I'm making great deals.

Sure I've worked hard to get here, but I'm also benefiting from the American Dream big time—as much as anybody ever has. I want it to continue. My theory of economics doesn't say that for me to do well you must do badly. Not everyone will be a success but everyone will have an equal chance to achieve it.

But to tell the whole truth, I'm worried too. Chances are you agree. With an election coming up next year there is the usual taking stock of where America stands and where we ought to be directing our energies. There are a lot of opinions out there that bother me, a lot of men running for office who don't seem cut out to be CEO of the USA. A number of these candidates have more than a few shortcomings.

Our current political system discourages truly capable men and women from seeking public office by forcing politicians to live in a fishbowl. A constant need for officeholders to grovel for campaign dollars means the smartest and most able business executives I know would never consider a bid for public office. Take Jack Welch, CEO of General Electric since 1981. To my mind, Welch has all the qualities to be a truly great president—toughness, incisiveness, honesty, and decisiveness. But a man of this quality will never run as long as our politics remains the special-interest cesspool that it has become.

Then there are single-issue candidates who are never going to see the big picture. There are candidates who've been in politics so long that they're not capable of telling you a straight story. One candidate, Pat Buchanan, believes we should reduce our commitments abroad, and I agree. But his startling view that the Western allies should not have stopped Hitler is repugnant. When he said that, he totally lost it. Hitler was a monster and it was essential for the allies to crush Nazism. To say that Hitler had no "malignant intentions" toward the United States is beyond belief. (Twenty years ago, Buchanan was less cautious. He called Hitler "an individual of great courage, a soldier's soldier . . . a leader steeped in the history of Europe," and talked about his other extraordinary gifts.) My grandfather was German. But I am proud of the vital role that the United States played in defeating the Third Reich. Buchanan denigrates the memory of those Americans who, in the Second World War, gave their lives in the effort to stop Hitler. Moreover, his remarks about Hitler suggest Buchanan would adopt a foreign policy today that is absolutely guaranteed to encourage the most oppressive, anti-American dictators in our own times.

Then there's Vice President Gore, an able, underrated man who seems confused these days. I hear he paid Naomi Wolf $15,000 to teach him how to be an alpha male. I could have gotten him Lenora Falani for much less. But then she defected to Buchanan.

Or consider the record of one of the supposedly brightest stars in the political sky: Bill Bradley. People treat him like he's about to give the updated version of the Sermon on the Mount. Let me tell you this about Bill Bradley: He's a disaster. He experimented with the tax code and cost thousands of people their jobs. Now he wants to be president, when in fact he quit the U.S. Senate because he could not get reelected.

Recently there have been some new names suggested for the presidency and one of them is mine. Minnesota governor Jesse Ventura has strongly encouraged me to run. I highly respect Jesse not only as a dynamic governor but also as the embodiment of the political qualities America needs. Given the choice between another slate of stale professionals and Jesse's mixture of basically common-sense principles and straight talk, it is no contest. He has convinced me that we need this same combination in the White House.

Even more persuasive to me are the polls. When the voters who actually plan to request Reform Party ballots are polled, I do very well. I also note that the Gallup–*USA Today*–CNN poll published in October showed that I would run a stronger race against George W. Bush and Al Gore than would Pat Buchanan—even though he has run for president three times and I am not even a candidate.

In another authoritative poll, running against George W. Bush and Al Gore I came in second, ahead of the vice president. Nobody ever accused me of modesty, but it's a tremendous honor to have millions of people considering you for high office when you didn't seek it out. And this isn't the first time my name has come up. In 1988 I was encouraged to seek the presidency. At various other times I've been asked to run for governor or mayor. There are plenty of signs that the country is looking for a candidate who comes from outside politics. In fact it's been looking for an outsider for some time.

I am definitely a different look. I'm not prepackaged. I'm not plastic. I'm not scripted. And I'm not "handled." I tell you what I think. It's quite a departure from the usual office-seeking pols. Maybe the voters would find it refreshing. I guarantee you one thing, they'd find it interesting. After two years of George W. Bush, John McCain, Al Gore, and Bill Bradley running for president, the voters will be bored to death. They'll be looking for a candidate who is straight-talking, straight-shooting, beholden to no one, and has proven that he can actually get things done.

Consider Governor Ventura. I met him when he appeared in some of the monster wrestling events I used to stage in Atlantic City. He was elected governor of Minnesota (knocking off a couple of old-time political pros) because he talks straight. Nonpoliticians like Ventura are the wave of the future. And it's going to be a lot easier for nonpoliticians to get elected to high office from here on out. Jesse may be the exception today, but straight-shooters like him will be the rule tomorrow. Voters are going to look to the worlds of business, entertainment, professional sports, and maybe the military—not to career politicians—for our next generation of political leadership. Remember the stir Colin Powell created merely by considering a run for high office.

Why are voters looking outside the political game for political players? The reason is that the American people want to be told the truth. They know we don't have the political leaders we deserve, and they know that if things don't change we won't have the America we deserve. Does that mean I have more faith in the people than the politicians do? I hope so, because a lot of people at the top of the political game think the American people are naive. They think the American people are like little kids who can't face facts.

Here's the bottom line: Any political leader who won't face the future head-on is putting the American Dream at risk. That dream has made this the best country in history. It's the dream my father and mother dreamed, the one they made come true for our family. It's the one that took me to the top. When you mess with the American Dream, you're on the fighting side of Trump.

STRAIGHT TALK

People want fresh answers. We have to look back a very long way to find private citizens speaking out and having a major impact on national affairs. We have to look back to the first days of the republic, to men like Washington, Jefferson, and Franklin, who had farms and businesses to run and who came to politics as ordinary citizens. They saw that things were out of control and that some clearer thinking was in order. (Let me say this right away to all eager reviewers: I'm not putting today's crop of politicians on the same level as the Founding Fathers. None of them would claim to be able to write the Declaration of Independence overnight, for example, the way Jefferson did. I'm not sure, on the other hand, how well Jefferson would handle a room full of foreign bankers—something I'm good at. Different people have different talents.)

A lot of Americans seem to want to cast a wider net in finding their leaders. It's worth remembering how many of this country's great leaders have come from outside the pool of Washington insiders. Reagan and Eisenhower, in our recent history, weren't politicians to begin with—and they turned out to be very good presidents. They both became successful by bringing personal experience and original thinking to old issues, and new management styles to problems that needed immediate attention. And we shouldn't forget that sixty years ago an almost unknown Wall Street lawyer and businessman named Wendell Willkie came from nowhere to grab the Republican presidential nomination and came within a whisker of being elected president. He was running against one of the most popular political figures in American history, Franklin Roosevelt.

Willkie was an interesting fellow. Born a poor boy in Indiana, he made a fortune in utilities and railroads. Willkie was actually a delegate to the 1936 Democratic Convention but Republicans nominated him for president just four years later, beating two tough competitors, Robert Taft and Tom Dewey.

How did Willkie do it? It seems he had the common touch. Even though he was a millionaire businessman he had a way of relating to the common man. He criticized the platforms of both Democrats and Republicans for "double talk, weasel words, and evasion."

The big media of the day—*Time, Life, Look, Colliers,* and the *New York Herald Tribune*—found Willkie fascinating. Overnight he was a major contender for the presidency.

Could it happen again? I think so.

My first reason for writing this book is that the American people want straight talk about politics. Whatever my ultimate decision about actively seeking the presidency, I'd encourage you to take the problems identified in this book and the solutions I propose and compare them with those of your favorite candidate. Keep score. I'm willing to bet that even when I seem most outside the box, I'm going to give you more straightforward, useful ideas than most of the guys getting the press and the interviews. Most politicians use language to conceal what they think. Or to conceal the fact that they don't think. Many are trained as lawyers and speak to win support rather than to define the truth. I use language to speak my mind. Being blunt hasn't hurt me so far. I've lived my life as I choose and said what I wanted to say.

FRED TRUMP AND FAMILY

My second reason for writing this book is more personal: Last summer my father, Fred Trump, died. He was ninety-three years old and, until five years ago when his memory began to fail, he came to the office every day. The reasons for my father's incredible career are actually pretty simple: He always worked faster and better and for less money than his competition. I learned much from him.

More important, he was intensely loyal and supremely positive. Whether I was building Trump Tower, the Trump Taj Mahal, or the Wollman Rink, he was always there for me. In the early '90s I owed banks billions and billions of dollars. My personal debt was $900 million. My father never once doubted me. He was as positive as ever. He'd tell anyone who asked about me, "Go back and bet the ranch on him." If he hadn't given that kind of support to me all my life I'm not sure I would have made it.

The day Pop died was the toughest day of my life. Mayor Giuliani was kind enough to say this at the funeral:

> Fred Trump not only helped to build our city, he helped to define it and to make it a very special city—the most famous city in the world—and he did it in the most important way possible: building homes for people. . . . He was the son of immigrants. . . . He helped to transform much of Brooklyn

and Queens and made safe, affordable homes available to middle-class New Yorkers whose work ethic is the backbone of our city. . . .

During the Depression, Fred Trump saw the need for affordable, quality housing, and he provided it. When the GIs returned from the Second World War, they found homes built by Fred Trump waiting to be occupied. Countless members of the baby-boom generation grew up in housing that Fred Trump built. . . .

Fred Trump was a very big man. . . . The success of this immigrant son and of his family stand as a symbol of the unlimited opportunities of all New Yorkers and all Americans.

Even this amazing review of his career doesn't begin to describe my father. He was the ultimate successful small businessman. He was a great husband for sixty-three years to my equally incredible mother. That's a record I'll never be able to equal. The lessons and gifts he gave his children made us strong, and he developed incredible working relationships throughout his life.

He was a very down-to-earth man. The day John F. Kennedy Jr. died, I received a note he'd written the day before. It said:

Dear Donald,

I read over the weekend of your father's passing and I just wanted to drop you a note. No matter where you are in life, losing a parent changes you. I know you had a close relationship and I hope you'll get ample time to reflect. He sounds like a fascinating man from what I read in the Times. I liked that he would go over his various worksites and pick up stray nails and return them to the carpenters. Clearly he never lost his perspective.

My condolences to you and your family.

Sincerely,

John Kennedy

If you read the obituaries on my father you'd have thought he had been a major statesman. People were deeply affected by his life. People, after all, feel strongly about their homes. Owning your own home is a big part of the American Dream. A man who provides so many homes to so many people has to seem a little bit superhuman.

To come to the point, I've taken John Kennedy's advice. I have reflected on my father and I realized, as many of you have, that when a father dies you begin to see yourself differently. It's up to you now to carry on the family business, the family tradition. You're the grown-up, one of the authorities in your family. You gain a new sense of responsibility. Those of us with experience, those of us with influence have an obligation to rebuild the world and make it a better place.

There are going to be readers of this who will ask about Trump's private life. Well, I've lived my life as an open book and I don't claim to be something I am not. What you see is what you would get. I've never taken drugs of any kind, never had a glass of alcohol. Never had a cigarette, never had a cup of coffee. I have been married twice and I have four wonderful kids. I'm now single and women seem to like me. Does that mean I don't value family relationships?

I haven't been as successful in my marriages as my parents were, but marriage is not the only family value that matters. The importance you give to your relationship with your kids is a family value. So is your relationship with your parents, your sisters and brothers, your feelings about the foods your family liked, the things you do for fun. A lot of people want to say that being monogamous is the only family value. They don't understand that family values means having a context, having a place where you belong, having people who really know you and to whom you're accountable.

A guy who was writing an article about me interviewed a few friends and business associates. He told me that the word "loyalty" kept coming up in these conversations. It's an important concept for me and among the people that I work with. One of the small corruptive forces in politics is the fact that every aide to every politician is hoping to retire on a tell-all book about his experiences as an insider. Loyalty counts for very little in Washington. I'd like to see it restored. Loyalty is a version of your love for your family. I feel loyalty not only to my friends but also to my city and my country. By my definition, one of the family values is patriotism.

THE COMING HEAVY WEATHER

I believe I have better hunches than most, but my place in the world has also given me better knowledge. My third reason for wanting to speak out is that I see not only incredible prosperity in our future but also the possibility of economic and social upheaval. Look toward the future and if you're like me you'll see storm clouds brewing. Big-time trouble. I'm not the only one who sees the storm on the horizon. A lot of people in public life and in private life know what may come our way. The politicians may not want to think about it but it's there.

The first storm—economic disaster: I hope I'm wrong, but I think we may be facing an economic crash like we've never seen before—probably sooner rather than later. The next president, or maybe the one we've got, could be in office for a stock market crash worse than the one in 1929. I'm not saying this crash will ruin us, but we have to anticipate it and know how to rebound. We'd better be ready, as a nation, to claw our way back up. Right now I'm not seeing the leadership we're going to need.

The second storm—terrorism: We need to get past the idea that, because we're the only superpower, we're safe. My uncle John Trump was an MIT professor and a brilliant man. He had a clear and compelling view of the future, including a strong belief that one day the United States might be subjected to a terrorist strike that would turn Manhattan into Hiroshima II. I always respected Uncle John, but sometimes found myself wondering if maybe he wasn't exaggerating just a bit.

Today we know that John Trump knew exactly what he was talking about.

So what are we doing about this threat? Are we getting tough with people who would wipe us out in a second? Hell, no.

Look at our policy toward North Korea, an outlaw, terrorist state run by a family of certifiable loons. If these guys don't scare you, you've been playing too many interactive games. North Korea has an army of goose-stepping maniacs, and they're building nuclear bombs while most of the population is starving to death. Think it through. What does it mean when the leadership of a country spends money on weapons instead of food for a starving population? Remember, starving populations have toppled more than one regime. If the North Korean rulers are exposing themselves to this kind of risk, you can be sure they're not building these weapons just for the hell of it. They're going to use them if they can.

We discovered this arms-building plan a couple of years ago. What did we do? We offered to build the North Korean government two light-water nuclear reactors and supply them with heating oil if they'd promise to be good. Am I the only one who thinks it might make more sense to disarm the North Korean nuclear threat before it shows up in downtown Seattle or Los Angeles?

It's time to look outward, and it's time for all of us who care about the American Dream to change the political buzz from happy talk to straight talk. Here's the bottom line: If a policy threatens the American Dream, we need to go after it.

I'm going to shoot straight about terrorism and about the foreign threat. I'm going to talk plain about the economy and how to keep the system solid at the core. If we do that, then we can ride out any storm. I'm also going to talk about Social Security. I'm lucky enough not to have to worry about getting a Social Security check, but most Americans do and they're right to be worried about their futures.

I'm also going to talk about the social issues that count to most Americans, especially education and what we need to do to get our schools back in shape. What amazes me about the education debate is that the kids are the last consideration. Their scores drop, their schools are unsafe, and the adults sit around worrying about job security and whether merit pay will hurt the self-esteem of the teachers who don't measure up.

My argument is simple. We put the kids first, every time, every way. We like to say that children are our future, but we're not treating them that way. I was reading a story about a kid in an inner city school. He didn't ask for much. He just wanted the doors locked so the punks couldn't come in off the streets and sell their drugs and shoot people who were trying to learn. This kid said he was scared to walk home. This is an American kid I'm talking about, and he's scared that he'll be shot at school. We send troops around the world to stamp out trouble, but we don't protect our own children. What about their American Dreams?

We must do everything we can to provide the best imaginable schools for our kids. A good friend of mine, Richard Kahan, has been working at developing new programs combining businesses with schools in New York. His program is training kids for real jobs in the contemporary marketplace. He points out that there is a $50-billion need to rebuild schools because all across the nation school buildings are deteriorating. Newly built schools can't be opened because of code violations. When kids go into buildings that are falling apart they get the picture: If these buildings are neglected, our education can't be really important; in fact, to adults, we're not important. Kids today should be given what kids got in the '20s, '30s, and '40s, and more. We should build schools that are attractive, that have adequate labs and computer facilities.

I'm a builder. I know how to work with (or against) bureaucracies. Richard Kahan is encouraging me to propose a massive rebuilding of the nation's schools. How would we pay for it? I ask. Richard says we could come up with $50 billion if we pulled our troops out of Europe. We can protect Europe with our nuclear arsenal and use those funds for schools.

My personal belief is that government can't handle a project of this size and complexity. But if you put together an alliance with labor and government, systematically doing away with government red tape, then maybe it would work. I'm thinking about it.

We definitely need to protect students. And we also need to let students and their parents decide which schools to patronize. Our GI Bill let a whole generation of Americans choose where to get their education, and I'd say it worked pretty well. We already know how to do it. School shootings, school dropouts all over the country tell us that the system isn't working. How many generations do we have to lose before we wise up?

Another big social issue I want to talk about is crime. Here's an area where strong leadership can change dark into light. I'm still having a hard time believing how safe New York has become, and it didn't get that way by accident. Mayor Giuliani has proved that commonsense policies backed up with a willingness to crack heads makes life better for everyone except the criminals. A lot of experts hounded Giuliani every step of the way, but he hung tough, hired some strong commissioners, and now people come to New York to feel safe—to actually get away from their smaller towns where criminals are still running wild.

If I were in charge of things, life would be even tougher for these predators. If there was a situation in New York like that terrible dragging death in Texas, I'd not only put the perpetrators to death, I'd find some way to make them an example to others.

If you're not tough on crime, then you're an enemy of the American Dream. The people who get hurt the most by crime aren't living in skyscrapers. They are, for the most part, living in poor neighborhoods. Crime keeps them from grabbing their part of the American Dream.

I have my eye on taxes and spending also. In my business, strict accounting can spell the difference between profit and loss. I have a lot of trouble with the way the government collects and handles our money. Hidden taxes make me mad as hell, and I'm not the only person who's had an objection to cost overruns. Most of all I object to the fact that this country is crippled economically by our national debt. I have a plan to pay off the national debt entirely, cut taxes on the middle class, repeal the inheritance tax, and save Social Security. It's a bold but realistic plan that can work—but no conventional politician would have the guts to propose it. You can read about it in chapter six.

And I've got some things to say about cleaning up politics, healthcare, and other concerns of mine. If you want straight talk, you're at the right address.

Because I've been successful, make money, get headlines, and have authored best-selling books, I have a better chance to make my ideas public than do people who are less well known. I have strong feelings that matters should be handled differently in our country and I'd like to see some things changed. But I'd consider this book a success if all I do is inspire other private citizens to begin thinking for themselves, bringing their own experiences and information to the political arena, and promoting their own answers to the problems we're just beginning to crash into. I want to democratize leadership in this country.

Several years ago John O'Donnell, who worked for me briefly and whom I fired, wrote a supposedly tell-all book in which he alleged that I made disparaging remarks about Blacks and Jews. This was a malicious attempt to smear me. Anyone who really knows me knows that I hate intolerance and bigotry.

My longtime involvement in promoting some of the biggest boxing events in history has allowed me to become friends with men like Muhammad Ali and Joe Frazier. Through them, and through more recent friendships with Puffy Combs, Sammy Sosa, and others, I've had the chance to learn firsthand about the diversity of American culture, and it has left me with little appetite for those who hate or preach intolerance.

One of our next president's most important goals must be to induce a greater tolerance for diversity. The senseless murder of Matthew Shepard in Wyoming—where an innocent boy was killed because of his sexual orientation—turned my stomach. We must work towards an America where these kinds of hate crimes are unthinkable.

There are some issues I don't want to say much about. I support a woman's right to choose, for example, but I am uncomfortable with the procedures.

When Tim Russert asked me on *Meet the Press* if I would ban partial-birth abortion if I were president, my pro-choice instincts led me to say no. After the show, I consulted two doctors I respect and, upon learning more about this procedure, I have concluded that I would indeed support a ban.

I have nothing to lose by expressing my opinions. There's nobody I have to please. I'm not counting on the financial support of anybody. Trump has one financial backer: Trump. Compare what I say with what your candidate is saying. Then decide whom you can trust.

Some people are going to say: Who is Donald Trump to talk about these big issues? What's his background? It's true that in my family we talked about real estate, not politics. But volunteering talents, being a good citizen has always been important to the Trump family. The charity work of my father, brother, and sister-in-law, and the judicial work of my sister, all point to that. We've benefited from the American Dream and we feel the duty to give back to the community. Those who don't are nothing more than parasites. When you look at who gives the largest proportion of their earnings to charity, it's often people at the lower end of the economic ladder. They've got a lesson to teach all of us. They're keeping the American Dream alive, and we're going to need them in the tough times.

It's true that I'm just a real estate guy, but as a private citizen I have the right to be heard. Let me tell you where, literally, I'm coming from.

I operate a lot of properties and run a lot of businesses. As much as possible, I like to know what's happening day to day. When I want to know how to improve a property I talk to someone who has been on-site for a while, who knows the ins and outs of the business on a daily basis. I talk to delivery men and cab drivers and waiters. But I realize that sometimes the person on top can get in the way. I've had guys in hard hats yell at me when I messed up their work while walking around a site. Once, when my ex-wife Ivana became overinvolved in the operations of one casino, a savvy manager began to call us with questions about every tiny detail. I got the point—delegate—and got off his back. This was a man who wanted to do his job right and was even willing to take on the boss; I love it when people who work for me care enough to take charge.

When I'm going into a new project I hire the best managers wherever I can find them. I pay them well. (I often scout my opponents. I've hired ex-government employees, for example, because they understand the workings of bureaucracy.) I've hired a number of women for high management positions, like Barbara Res, the first woman ever put in charge of a skyscraper in New York. A lot of people, including my sister Maryanne Trump Barry, who was just appointed a judge of the third district court, will tell you that hiring my assistant, Norma Foerderer, who has worked for me since about 1980, is one of the best decisions I ever made.

I like to think that I learned from my father how to hire the right people. Many employees who worked for him were there for twenty, thirty, or forty years. My brother Robert, who doesn't miss anything, says about Pop, "He knew how to pick them and how to keep them." His secretary, Amy Luerssen, was indispensable. (If I try to match the old man, I'll have to offer Norma a fifty-year contract. Not a bad plan.)

I put people together for their management skills, but I like to find good combinations as well. And when I feel that I have the right team, I let them show me what they can do.

In the early '90s, when the bottom fell out of the real estate market, I believe I survived because of the people I assembled. I was $9.2 billion in debt, $900 million of which was in personal guarantees. It was an amazing experience. One night in 1991, in front of Tiffany's with an friend, I saw a man with a seeing-eye dog and pencils in a can. I pointed him out. "Do you realize that man is worth $900 million more than I am," I said to her. "I'm worth minus $900 million right now."

How did I turn things around? I hired Nick Ribis to oversee my casino operations. Ribis is one of the toughest, most hardworking, and best-organized executives I know. I brought other new people into my New York office, including Steve Bollenbach, who is now the top executive at Hilton and one of the most brilliant guys I know. We worked hard together. Through my own efforts and those of others, I not only climbed out of that abyss but also built my businesses back to something several times as valuable. Now I own 40 Wall Street, a number of other buildings around Manhattan, and the land under the Empire State Building. You know about Atlantic City: Trump Marina, Trump Taj Mahal, and Trump Plaza. Nick has said about me that what saved the Trump Organization at that time was my willingness to step back, not to be too hands-on, and to let the talented people who work for me do their own thing.

I've taken the same approach in refining my political agendas in the writing of this book. I've talked to people who seemed to have the right talent, energy, and ideas. I've read widely until I found authors who saw problems the way I do and proposed solutions that make sense. I've based my political programs on this research and these conversations. But I'm also bringing a perspective to politics that most politicians don't have. I've built a multibillion-dollar empire by using my intuition. Here, I'm letting my instincts tell me how we have to work together to build the America we deserve. What I stand for is quality of work. I stand for getting things done.

Besides that, what makes the political pros and Washington insiders believe that they have an edge on the truth? Think for a second about what the entire political world was obsessing over throughout 1998 and part of 1999: Monica. I think the national consciousness has been deeply scarred. Americans have been drained of their spirit by the entire Clinton-Lewinsky impeachment fiasco. I think the voters want both Clintons offstage and want to put the whole sordid mess behind us. That's what they mean by Clinton fatigue. When confronted with the Lewinsky matter, Clinton should have stoutly refused to discuss his private life. He should also have declined to answer, rather than perjure himself. If the Clinton affair proves anything it is that the American people don't care about the private lives and personal affairs of our political leaders so long as they are doing the job.

I got a chuckle out of all the moralists in Congress and in the media who expressed public outrage at the president's immoral behavior. I happen to know that one U.S. senator leading the pack of attackers spent more than a few nights with his twenty-something girlfriend at a hotel I own. There's also a conservative columnist, married, who was particularly rough on Clinton in this regard. He also brought his girlfriend to my resorts for the weekend. Their hypocrisy is amazing.

★   ★   ★

I'm not worried about whether or not the intellectual/journalistic/ political establishment thinks I've got the stuff to talk about saving the American Dream. I believe in the American Dream. My business experience shows me that it works, and I want to do everything possible to see that regular Americans can enjoy the same opportunity for success and security that I have had. That means the American Dream unencumbered by bureaucratic ineptitude, government regulation, confiscatory tax policies, racism, discrimination against women, or discrimination against people based on sexual orientation. We must all have equal access to the American Dream. It's a dream we deserve and a dream worth fighting for.

CHAPTER ONE

The Business of America Is Business

IF WE RUN INTO HARD times we need to know what resources we have, which systems work and which don't. I'd say up front that what's worked beautifully throughout American history is the free-market economy. What has brought us low is government bureaucracy and corruption.

There are a number of monuments to the American Dream. Some would list Mount Rushmore and the Washington Monument. Others would suggest the traditional family home, Sunday dinners, happy children playing in the backyard. But my personal favorite is the New York skyline—the big, brassy picture that comes to the minds of people all over the world when you mention America. From the Statue of Liberty to the World Trade Center to the Empire State Building, the buildings of New York tell the story of our country—the American Dream in stone and glass.

Why? Because New York has seen the best of times and the worst of times, and whatever happens it always comes out a little

brighter and a few stories higher. New York is for me the most daz-
zling example of the American Dream at work. The lessons it
teaches—lessons of hope, opportunity, struggle, and accomplish-
ment—can help support us through the good times and sustain us
when hard times come.

And hard times probably are coming. The current wisdom sees no
further than the latest stock market rally. Our feel-good community
seems to think the economic laws of gravity have been suspended.
But the fact is that throughout history what went up always came
down. I talked in the introduction about the storms on our horizon.
Let me give you a couple of reasons why I see hard times ahead. Then
we'll get into the specifics of what we need to do to protect and continue the American Dream.

First off, as I said, I really am convinced we're in danger of the
sort of terrorist attacks that will make the bombing of the Trade
Center look like kids playing with firecrackers. No sensible analyst
rejects this possibility, and plenty of them, like me, are not wondering
if but *when* it will happen. Nor is there any doubt that when people
are under attack, or fear societal mayhem of any type, their priorities
are not on investing. Their minds are going to be on digging in and
surviving, and this attitude will have major economic consequences.

Second, even without this sort of disaster, I believe we're in
danger of a financial downturn because we've gone so high so fast.
You can hear this opinion expressed by top business leaders, though
they may not run around crying out that the sky is going to fall,
because it could be a self-fulfilling prophesy. And you hear it as well
from private citizens who've kept their eyes open. There is a growing

consensus that our dizzying prosperity will sputter. Economists long ago recognized the phenomenon of business cycles. Business schools, such as my alma mater, Wharton, taught that economics was cyclical.

But when was the last time you heard a major politician warning of economic downturn? It's just not in the vocabulary of any public figure. Except mine.

The reason most politicians don't predict a slump is that they don't understand it. More to the point, they have no solutions. I'm positive enough to know that if we play our cards right we can get through even the worst of times. America has survived econimic disaster in the past. So have I.

Consider the current budget surplus. The Democrats want to spend all of it, using some of it to pay down the national debt. The Republicans want to give it all back in the form of deep tax cuts. They're both wrong . . . and right. Now, in a period of prosperity, is the time to hedge against the economic hard times ahead. Both debt reduction *and* tax reduction are key and necessary. I'd rather have the people spend their money than have the government spend it. But typical of the polarized politics of Washington, both parties demand all or nothing. The proper course is to use a portion of the surplus and still provide meaningful tax cuts for working families—not for the guys in my bracket. That is the art of compromise. This course of action now will prepare us for the economic downturn ahead by reducing the government's interest payments and by allowing families to save more in preparation for the lean times ahead. But you don't hear compromise and dealmaking from Washington. Maybe it's time we had a president who was a dealmaker.

Consider this: There are companies that came out of nowhere a couple of years ago and now are worth tens of billions of dollars. If Amazon.com merged with Warner Bros., Amazon, whose directors say they have yet to make a profit, would be the majority party. Incredible, but true. Then there's eBay.com, the on line auction house, which has grown 1900 percent in four years. That sounds impressive, but wild rises like this indicate instability. Like a bipolar personality, there are high highs in the economy and then come the lows. I've seen this in real estate—prices going up through the ceiling, then suddenly crashing through the floor. These changes are made even more dramatic by modern technology. You have to remember that it's very easy these days for investors to move money around the globe. When the tide turns, investor support can shift at the speed of light. The magic carpet can unravel very quickly.

I am convinced the American people are sick of gridlock—the logjam of two parties in Washington so opposed to each other that the people's business doesn't get done. Perhaps it is time for a deal-maker, a leader who can get the leaders of Congress to the table, forge consensus, strike compromise, and get things done. That's how we will get real tax relief, Social Security reform, healthcare reform, and campaign finance reform.

With all due respect, that's my strength, it's what I do. Many times I've achieved results when others said it was impossible. I believe I could be most effective for the American people.

OUR NEXT COMEBACK

America will stage a comeback, and our next comeback must be led by people who know what works and what doesn't. That's why the

New York story is so valuable. It is a story of people from all over our country and, in fact, all over the world—people who started out with next to nothing and ended up kings.

When you think of American heroes, the names that come to mind are almost always those of politicians or soldiers. Our teachers overlook some of the most dynamic parts of our heritage by not honoring businesspeople as well. A lot of them have had extremely interesting lives, full of drama. They not only grabbed the brass ring for themselves, but also created jobs and opportunities for countless other people. If I were in the movie business, I'd do films about some of these people. If we have movies about gangsters, hookers, and cannibals, why not movies about business heroes who built the greatest country in history? If businesspeople were more widely celebrated, maybe their opinions might be taken more seriously.

Look around New York City and you'll find a blockbuster success story on every block: The W. R. Grace Company skyscraper, named for an Irish kid who came to New York with big ambitions. The Waldorf Astoria, built by Conrad Hilton, a dreamer who started his career in the family hotel in San Antonio, New Mexico. Rockefeller Center, built by the heirs of the legendary John D. Rockefeller. There are important New York landmarks commemorating Cornelius Vanderbilt, Marcus Goldman, Meyer Guggenheim, Andrew Carnegie, Nathan Handwerker, and others. If you look around your own community you'll see the same thing: landmarks left by people with vision and determination, people who literally made something out of nothing.

As I've already said, my father was cut from the same cloth. Fred Trump was born in New Jersey in 1905. His father, who came here from Germany as a child, was as big and brash as any character from a Jack London novel. He went to Alaska for the Gold Rush. He owned a hotel there. After he came back east, his wife, Elizabeth, ran the family business. My grandfather Trump died when Dad was eleven years old. In those days you didn't hoof it down to the welfare line when hard times hit, you hit the bricks looking for work. At eleven years old, my father became the family breadwinner, delivering fruit, shining shoes, hauling lumber on a construction site. Nothing fancy—the kind of work that people avoid in droves these days. But my dad knew something that we too often forget: There is opportunity in adversity. Call it a cliché if you want, but I'm here to tell you that it's also the truth—and we'd better never forget it.

Dad never gave up and he kept his eyes open for opportunity. Early in his high school years he discovered a talent for the precise geometry of construction. He wasn't a skyscraper guy, but he did build his first structure at age sixteen—a two-car frame garage for a neighbor. Pretty soon he was building prefabricated garages for fifty dollars apiece, and not long after that he was building single-family homes in Queens. When I think of Dad helping other Americans realize their part of the Dream—and let's never forget that home ownership is at the heart of the American Dream—I feel as proud as any son ever felt about his father.

His secret was really no secret at all. He worked hard his whole life. And he looked for opportunity even when you would think opportunity had vanished. When the Depression hit, for example, he bought a bankrupt mortgage company and sold it at a profit a year later. Next he built a self-service supermarket in Woodhaven, one of the first of its kind. All the local tradesmen—butcher, tailor, shoe-maker—rented concessions in the space. It was convenient, a natural success. There are many, many similar success stories in this city's history, but the point is this: None of these guys started out from the top. They started small. They grew tall. They stand as examples to all of us.

There are great success stories from today's news as well: Bill Gates, Steve Jobs, and the others who created the computer revolution; entertainment figures like Steven Spielberg, Ted Turner, Madonna, Michael Jordan, Bill Cosby, and Oprah Winfrey. I wish this list were even longer. I wish more people in America were famous for their remarkable successes. I'm afraid our system has prevented many from being everything they might be and giving everything they might give.

Ronald Reagan once said, in America our origins matter less than our destinations. I'm not saying that everyone makes it—not even the bright and talented. Sometimes there's too much to overcome, too much adversity. Kids who are raised in violent neighborhoods, without parents, don't have the chance they ought to have. Many good, bright people never make it because of illness, bad planning, bad luck, or other purely personal reasons. The bars and crack houses of New York are full of the disappointed. And some choose to achieve goals that don't signify success to everybody. There are artists and teachers and police officers and clergy, and other wonderful Americans who didn't choose their careers to become rich and famous. But they've had a chance to live their dream.

We have to do everything possible to keep the dream machine alive. When we hit hard times, we must protect the heart of our system— opportunity—from the people who will panic and demand that government bureaucrats run the show. And even in the best of times, we need to make sure there are as few obstacles as possible to realizing one's full potential. This takes us into the political world, where there are many good people but, unfortunately, some very bad ideas.

OUTPLANNING THE PLANNERS

Most of us think the American Dream is a birthright, but I've been around long enough to realize that, without constant care and vigilance, it can and will be whittled down to nothing. The threatening agent is not some foreign power, but people who don't understand the proper relationship between the public and private arenas. In other words, the greatest threat to the American Dream is the idea that dreamers need close government scrutiny and control. Job one for us is to make sure the public sector does a limited job, and no more.

Mayor Giuliani summed it up pretty well: "Government should not and cannot create jobs through government planning. The best it can do, and what it has a responsibility to do, is to deal with its own finances first, to create a solid budgetary foundation that allows businesses to move the economy forward on the strength of their energy and ideas." He was talking about New York, but what he said is true for America.

The next mayor should stick with Giuliani's basic prescription: Provide everyone with a good, free education and clean, well-stocked libraries. Make sure the streets are safe. Ensure reasonable regulation, but no more.

It's no secret, however, that for much of this century government has been falling down on the basics, while sometimes becoming excessively involved in areas where it should play a restricted role. It has allowed criminals to have the run of the streets and the subways. Instead of putting the arm on criminals, government at all levels has saddled businessmen and women with ridiculous, dream-killing regulations. We are better off today than we were even a few years ago, thanks to a new breed of politician that recognized the problems that high taxes and rampaging regulations were causing. But if we forget what has happened in the past, we will be doomed to relive it in the future.

I will never forget the 1970s, when reckless regulators were running the show—make that horror show. New York City had a near-death experience when the city budget failed under Mayor Beame. Municipal bonds were worth less than Confederate money. You'd think that experience would have served as a wake-up call. But under Mayors Ed Koch and David Dinkins things went steadily downhill. I thought Dave Dinkins was a decent and well-meaning guy, but the absurdity of those times is preserved in the Kummerfeld Report, which was put together by a "blue-ribbon panel" commissioned by the mayor. This group looked for ways to deal with the enormous and dangerous budget deficit that New York faced in 1993. My teeth still chatter when I think of the "solutions" they came up with.

In order to protect city finances, the report recommended firing city workers. It suggested an increase in the real property tax for owners of single-family homes. It proposed an increase in the city's sales tax, already sky-high, and tolls for all of the East River and Harlem River bridges. The commission also recommended a residential garbage-collection fee, a tax on movie and theater tickets, the elimination of scheduled police hires, and cutting subsidies for day care. If you had to boil down the operating philosophy to a couple of lines, it would be something like this: Life is getting worse in New York. It is too costly and too dangerous. This decline in the quality of life is driving people out of the city and into the suburbs, which in turn is cutting into our tax base and blowing up the budget. So what should we do? Let's make life in the city even more costly and more dangerous!

This is a classic example of a cure that kills the patient. It is sort of like calling in a doctor and looking up to see the Grim Reaper coming through the door. People often make bad decisions in panic situations; hard times often create panic. It's important to remind ourselves, during good times, which steps we need to take and which to avoid when things are bad.

Like so many politicians across America, the old guard suffered from the illusion that tax cuts would only make things worse—which in fact is an illusion that remains popular among some political leaders. No one considered that encouraging people to move back into the city would actually generate the revenue needed to balance the budget. Nor did this commission understand that when the private sector expands, even the simplest projects become impossible. Let me give an example that still boggles my mind.

In my first book, *The Art of the Deal,* I described the fight I had to wage to persuade the city government to allow me to rebuild the city-owned Wollman skating rink in Central Park—at my own expense. My offer to help was opposed for one reason only: City Hall knew that if I took on the job, the difference between my work and the job the city was doing would expose the incompetence of city government. Once I finally embarrassed Mayor Koch and other city officials into letting me do it, even I was shocked at just how ridiculously incompetent the Koch administration turned out to be.

Here's a comparison to keep in mind: It took me two and a half years to build the sixty-eight-story Trump Tower—one of the most beautiful and distinctive skyscrapers in the world. Yet for six years the city bungled, bobbled, and botched the job of fixing a no-story municipal skating rink. They let a year go by before drawing up time plans and completing the bidding process. The Parks Department redesigned the rink on a pitch, so that at the deep end the water might not freeze completely and skaters might fall through. This would then have become the only municipal skating rink in the modern world that would need a lifeguard station.

Falling through the ice was a real possibility. Instead of choosing a proven cooling technology, the city chose an exotic and experimental method to cool the ice. When they finally got the delicate copper pipes in place, what did they do? Left them exposed to the elements for nine months. Then they made a disaster of laying the concrete and ruined the pipes again, this time with jackhammers. When all was said and done, we had "the mother of all skating-rink debacles." This led to a fifteen-month study of what had gone wrong. This was, don't forget, the same administration you had to deal with if you wanted to do business in New York. We might shake our heads over the bad planning in impoverished soviet satellite countries, but for a while it seemed as though my hometown was in the same league.

When the city finally let me step in, I got the job done in four months flat, $750,000 under budget, and a full month ahead of schedule. In just three construction days, we managed to lay twenty-two miles of pipe. I had the time of my life running this rescue operation and, more important, I learned from this experience just how hard it is for normal, sane, earnest Americans to make their dreams come true when they have to confront mule-headed, but powerful, burons—a buron being defined as a cross between a bureaucrat and a moron. Nice expression, I think.

To me, the Wollman Rink and the Kummerfeld Report are perfect examples of the buronic arts—a combination of arrogance and incompetence that has depopulated cities around America, and which we need to fight any time we see them in action. Philadelphia and Boston are now at their lowest populations since 1900. St. Louis now has as many people as it had in the days of Mark Twain. People come to cities, check out the business climate, and all too often have the same response: Get us out of here. The result is devastating for urban dwellers, especially those who need better jobs to move into the ranks of the middle class.

We should never underestimate the degree to which burons can screw up other peoples' lives. An article I read by Ronald D. Utt said it best:

> After more than thirty years of federal involvement and the expenditure of more than half a trillion dollars of state and federal urban revitalization money, it is becoming increasingly apparent that [a] vast array of federal programs not only failed to bring the cities any relief, but may well have been an important contributing factor in the acceleration of their decline.

The article also quotes Indianapolis mayor Stephen Goldsmith: "Federal urban policy drives wealth out of our cities. In fact, if we specifically designed a 'suburban policy' to drive investment out of our cities, it would look a lot like our current system."

What characterized New York is still the case in Washington, D.C., and other major cities as well: high taxes, money wasted and misspent on public works projects, potholes big enough for sumo wrestlers to disappear into, and streets that have battlefield casualty rates. This collection of urban pathologies was perfectly described in the 1960s in *The Death and Life of Great American Cities,* by Jane Jacobs, a prominent expert on cities:

> . . . low income projects that become worse centers of delinquency, vandalism and general social hopelessness than the slums they were supposed to replace. . . . Cultural centers that are unable to support a good bookstore. Civic centers that are avoided by everyone but bums, who have fewer choices of loitering place than others. Commercial centers that are lackluster imitations of standardized suburban chain store shopping. Promenades that go from no place to nowhere and have no promenaders. Expressways that eviscerate great cities. This is not the rebuilding of cities. This is the sacking of cities.

That's a pretty dramatic analysis, but I believe it's true. I know that defenders of these policies are saying, "We meant well." But the time is long past for us, as a nation, to accept the "good intentions" dodge when major mistakes have been committed. In real life, intentions really don't matter—results are what count. And we know what works and what doesn't. We should have a zero-tolerance policy for people who advocate discredited regulatory schemes. They had their chance, and they produced a debacle. In my opinion, these people are opportunity destroyers. They're guilty of what I call Dreamicide.

BEYOND BURONICS

Let me talk a minute about how regulations have ambushed—and continue to ambush—businesses, and especially the smaller firms that do most of the dream-weaving in this country.

Small businesses sustain America's great middle class, without which we cannot survive. Two out of every three new jobs in the United States are created by small and medium-sized businesses. A majority of new small-business owners are women. More than 80 percent of all business establishments employ fewer than twenty people. Small business is the heart, soul, and beauty of the American economy. We have tens of thousands of entrepreneurs, all with an idea, putting together a business and hiring ten or fifteen people. This is the glory of our system, and also its strength. Don't get me wrong. Small business is a hard road, and a lot of these firms ultimately fail. But to my mind, these small-business owners are American heroes. It's our responsibility to make sure the system isn't stacked against them. It's our obligation to make sure that small businesses aren't crushed and that hard work is rewarded.

In my casino business I deal with hundreds of small businesses selling me everything from linens to computer terminals. I search for small, well-managed companies who provide solid service. This is how big business helps small business—and vice versa.

Supporting small business is not always easy, however, for this reason: The burons are like weeds—you spray them, you burn them out, you pour concrete over top of them, but give them a few weeks and they'll be back. Small-business people are definitely feeling the pain that government bureaucracies are creating.

In 1995 the White House convened a conference with more than 1,600 representatives of small businesses. When asked what their highest priorities were for federal action, the vast majority ranked paperwork reduction and regulation at the top. No wonder. As even the Small Business Administration admits, "small-business owners often fear that they will inadvertently fail to comply with some obscure rule and that a government inspector will show up, close down the business, and drive them into bankruptcy. Many believe, with some justification, that the government is more interested in obtaining penalties than in promoting compliance with the law."

"With justification" is right. When dealing with regulation, a Fortune 500 company can afford to unleash its lawyers and accountants and they often bend things their way. The small entrepreneur is not so lucky. His or her margin is too thin to pass on the costs of attorney and accountant fees to the customer. And he or she is all but powerless against the hordes of inspectors that eat away at small business like locusts. I'm willing to bet that burons have destroyed more small businesses than has whiskey.

For a country that has such an excess of regulation, by the way, it's interesting that we often don't regulate the right businesses. Think about whiskey. I don't know why everyone's suing tobacco companies—though they're terrible—and leaving alcohol companies alone. I lost a brother to alcohol. (I've never had a drink in my life because of my older brother Fred Jr.'s trouble with alcohol. He was handsome, brilliant, the nicest guy in the world. But he got into alcohol and it destroyed his life.) You have terrible auto accidents because of alcohol, thousands killed. Taxing alcohol companies isn't enough; I'd like to see them forced to take responsibility. And I'd continue to go after tobacco. Tobacco is a drug. It ultimately destroys your lungs and your insides. The tobacco companies ought to pay for the consequences.

You don't have to be an entrepreneur to feel the pinch or regulation. Each American, whatever he or she does, spends more than forty workdays just to pay the costs of federal rules. The total cost of government has been estimated, I'm told, at $3.38 trillion, nearly $1 trillion of which results from federal and state regulation. In all, the federal government is responsible for imposing more than $2,800 in regulatory costs for every man, woman, and child in America.

Apparently that's not enough to satisfy its eternal appetite. Despite all the talk out of Washington about reinventing government, the monster grows larger and larger. I've had the figures checked and here are a few that should make you nervous:

In 1970 the Federal Register was 20,036 pages long. During the eight-year presidency of Ronald Reagan the number of pages declined by more than 22,642—from an all-time high of 73,258 under President Carter. It is now inching its way back up toward 70,000 pages. The Code of Federal Regulations, an annual listing of executive agency regulations published in the Federal Register, includes all regulations now in effect. In 1996 the CFR filled 204 volumes with a total of 132,112 pages. It takes nineteen feet of shelf space just to hold it all. According to the General Accounting Office, from 1996 to 1998 federal regulatory agencies issued 8,675 final rules and sent them to Congress for review. A full 125 were defined as "major" rules—rules that will have an annual effect on the economy of more than $100 million. How the hell is a guy who is trying to start up a pizzeria going to cope with all that paper?

I'm not one of those guys who lives in the wilds and says we don't need any regulations. Of course we need some. But we've got to seek a reasonable level, and stick with it.

Let me give an example of how unchecked regulations can get out of hand—this example hits very close to home. The National

THE BUSINESS OF AMERICA IS BUSINESS

Association of Homebuilders estimates that the regulatory costs of building a house in three typical metropolitan areas of the United States tripled between 1974 and 1994. Like kudzu, this sort of damaging and explosive regulatory growth must be killed. Otherwise we're going to need to get a hall pass before we can go to the bathroom in our own homes.

Not only are there too many regulations, but some of them are also crazy. We all know examples. Here are a few of my favorites: In 1993 Northwest Airlines caused quite a stir when it rehired a fired pilot as a ground trainer. What had people rattled? Three years earlier, this pilot had been fired for flying a planeload of people after an all-night drinking binge that left his blood alcohol level somewhere between stewed and pickled. But under regulations mandated by the Americans with Disabilities Act, Northwest was forced to rehire him. In the eyes of the law he wasn't irresponsible, he was a man with a disability.

When it comes to real disabilities I don't think tolerance even enters the picture. Of course you help people who have been dealt a tough hand. But let's think clearly. Nobody made this pilot get drunk. He picked up the bottle on his own and got drunk on his own. Why does that make him qualify as a person with a disability? Maybe his drinking was caused by the disease of alcoholism (which, as I've said, claimed a member of my family as it has many of yours). Then his company should have forced him to seek treatment. The fact is, I have my own plane and if the government told me I had to put a known drunk on my flight crew, I'd refuse. Vehemently. A sick pilot's rights don't include the right to endanger me or my family or my friends.

You see these sorts of abuses everywhere. Under Michigan's "discrimination law," a jury, citing narcolepsy as a protected category, awarded $610,000 to a narcoleptic surgeon. Narcolepsy, by the way, is a condition that causes people to fall asleep at the blink of an eye. Do we really want doctors nodding off in the middle of surgery?

The U.S. Equal Employment Opportunity Commission should be in the business of protecting African Americans, Hispanics, Gays, and other minorities against obvious discrimination. Instead, it spends its time on a lot of stupid stuff, like filing a suit against Federal Express for its policy of employing only drivers with sight in both eyes, the same standard that the U.S. Department of Transportation uses. The EEOC regards it as unlawful to forbid one-eyed drivers from operating big rigs. Television shows and magazines like *Reader's Digest* run stories like these all the time. Keep your eyes open for them. They show you in detail our democracy in action.

Add it all up and here's what you've got: Thanks to excessive regulation, your next pilot could be drunk at the stick, your next surgeon might be asleep on the scalpel, and the driver of the eighteen-wheeler in the next lane may have a bit of a seeing problem.

My experience has been in fighting bureaucracy in cities. But regulation can mess up lives in rural settings as well.

I just read about the case of Taung Ming-Lin, a Taiwanese immigrant who bought land in Kern County, California, on which he planned to grow Chinese vegetables for sale to Southern California's Asian community. Lin says the county told him the land was already zoned for farming and that no permit was needed. But when Lin began farming, the government alleged that his tractor disturbed the habitat of the endangered Tipton kangaroo rat. It also alleged that Lin's tractor ran over some of the rats. Lin was charged with federal civil and criminal violations of the Endangered Species Act.

Lin speaks no English. He suffered a stroke shortly after being charged. The criminal charges carried penalties of up to a year in jail and a $100,000 fine. (Neighboring farmers started a defense fund, and the charges were later dropped.) Through an interpreter, Lin said, "One half of me is relieved. The other half says I never made a mistake."

Well, both halves of me say Enough!

These regulations begin with the assumption that hardworking, thrifty people deserve to be treated like common criminals. And they are all but designed to kill jobs and opportunity. Regulations tend to kick in when a company hires a certain number of people—some start when the number of employees reaches fifteen or twenty, while a cluster of regulations takes effect when a company hires its fiftieth employee. Now ask yourself, if you own a small company are you going to hire that fifteenth person? That twentieth person? That fiftieth person?

You'd be crazy.

Blaming bureaucrats is easy. Every election has hundreds of candidates who bash the bureaucracy. When they take office, lo and behold, they discover that the bureaucrats are more powerful than they thought. Or it becomes clear that playing along with bureaucracy can be personally very rewarding.

Blaming others, even when they deserve it, isn't enough because it doesn't show us how to take charge of problems ourselves. I think there's something else that encourages city construction workers in New York to kill time while my casino workers in New Jersey generally work their tails off: self-interest. The employees of Trump casinos know that if they do a good job they'll be promoted. They also know that their city will prosper if the casinos stay there and that it will die if the casinos leave.

Before I took over the Wollman Rink job I happened to walk by the construction site twice in one day. I noticed, in the morning, one worker who seemed to be on break. In the afternoon he was also on break and it looked as though it was the same long break he'd begun in the morning. This guy may simply have been lazy, but for sure he was out of touch. He was working for a company that was working for city inspectors who were working for mid-level bureaucrats who were beholden to the city lawyers and city inspectors and overseen by city government. He'd lost track of the fact that his real employer was the citizens of New York and that he was one of them. He was building (or supposed to be building) a skating rink, a public facility—something he and his family might enjoy. He was working for himself. If that had been made clear to him and the rest of his crew, I have to believe that self-interest alone would have sped up the job.

When you look at your favorite political candidate don't just look at his or her program. Find out what that candidate knows about motivating people. See how he or she has performed when running a staff.

The good news is that whenever things get so far out of hand, common sense comes back into play. All that's needed to fix what's wrong with government is to get it back to its limited, but vital, mission.

Ronald Reagan had the right idea, and more recently Mayor Giuliani put the same idea into play. Instead of raising taxes, he cut the costs of living in New York by $1.1 billion in tax reform and reduction. He saved small landlords a half billion dollars in the area of commercial rent alone, and slashed the paperwork burden of compliance. He implemented a co-op and condo abatement program that has saved owners about $100 million.

As the mayor was cutting taxes, the city budget swelled with revenue. The housing stock is in better shape than it's been in decades. Mayor Giuliani worked closely with Governor George Pataki to reduce the hotel occupancy tax, then the highest in the country. The result, not surprisingly, has been a resounding return of New York as one of America's premier convention sites. The hotel business, I am pleased to report, is hotter than ever.

Using the old Koch-Dinkins-Kummerfeld approach, the city should have lost money. In reality, after the hotel occupancy tax was cut, the city got a boost of almost $50 million more in tax revenue.

The sales tax in New York is sky-high at 8.25 percent. After lobbying for three years, the mayor got Albany to allow "back to school" sales-tax-free weeks in September for clothing under $100. There was also a one-week exemption period in January for clothing and footwear sales for items of less than $500. The old Koch-Dinkins-Kummerfeld line would be that the city could only lose money. In fact the city is making money because of record business revenues. People used to go to the suburbs just to shop. Now folks from Newark to White Plains are shopping again in the city.

Mayor Giuliani also returned $100 million to local entrepreneurs by cutting the unincorporated business tax. "We inaugurated targeted tax cuts aimed at freeing business from government regulation," Mayor Giuliani says. "At the same time, working cooperatively with the city's labor unions, we reduced the size of government, without layoffs, to begin to mitigate the distorting effects of having a government that is far too large an employer in relation to the private sector."

What's the bottom line? I have the figures in front of me.

Between 1994 and 1996 New York City gained almost 21,000 jobs in the tourism and restaurant business. New York has gained 178,000 private wage and salary jobs, reversing the Dinkins administration's loss of 320,000 private sector jobs. In fact the increase in private sector jobs in New York over the last four years has been the highest annual percentage increase in the city's history, with vigorous job growth in all five boroughs. Job creation in New York is more diverse, with growth shifting from finance and insurance to retail trade, media and entertainment, services and construction. Welfare reform in New York has encouraged more than 300,000 welfare recipients to leave the public assistance rolls over the past three years. The mayor has made it clear that the process of welfare reform in New York is just getting started.

What has worked in New York can work elsewhere. And it is working. Until recently, Indianapolis was another great American city in decline. Under the leadership of Mayor Goldsmith, the city has reduced operating expenses, cut its bureaucracy by 26 percent, reduced red tape, balanced the budget, cut property taxes, put more police officers on the streets, and invested $1.1 billion in the largest infrastructural improvement program in the city's history. Moreover, the local economy has enjoyed four consecutive years of record-setting investment and new jobs.

Indianapolis spends half the money that Washington, D.C., spends per resident. And yet, by any standard, taxpayers get a result that is incalculably better.

The crime and murder rates in Indianapolis are well below the big-city average, its unemployment rate is the lowest of all the big cities and well below the national average, and its poverty rate is just below the national average—making it the only eastern or mid-western city to achieve this distinction.

Drive through Indianapolis if you have the chance. Because I own a casino riverboat in Gary, Indiana, I've been to Indianapolis and I'm impressed. Take a walk downtown. Things are happening. Parents are out pushing their strollers. Buildings are going up. It's almost as if the air were better. Energy comes to a place when the economic climate is right.

Elsewhere, mayors like Richard Riordan of Los Angeles, reform-minded governors like Tommy Thompson of Wisconsin and John Engler of Michigan, have tried similar commonsense approaches to economic development and welfare policy. Wherever leaders have put results before process, the results have been astounding. They make sure the system rewards those who produce and they screen out those who make no contribution. They let money stay in the hands of people who earn it. They've simplified regulations. And they've stepped back and let human ambition and ingenuity take its course.

In 1996 Congress followed the example set by these mayors and governors by passing the Personal Responsibility and Work Opportunity Reconciliation Act. From now on, in America, the emphasis for able-bodied people is on getting a job. And Washington is finally giving the states and cities the freedom to experiment, to seek the best ways to get people back to work. That's what they want and we should do whatever we can to help them. Since the act went into effect in 1996, welfare caseloads dropped by 2.2 million. In all, it has dropped by more than 4.4 million since 1994, when several states implemented successful demonstration programs. As a result of these reforms, for the first time in twenty-five years, welfare caseloads across the country now contain fewer than ten million people.

The laws of human nature and the guidance of common sense tell us that the two basic principles of governing should work anywhere they are applied.

First: Get government out of skating rinks and any other activities it can't do well. (A list, by the way, of things government doesn't do well is a very long list.)

Second: Get government back in the business of providing for public convenience (transportation, public works) and safety (police and firefighters), and make sure that it does so efficiently. Then judge its effort by visible, definable results and fine-tune as needed.

Again, if government can do its job, the people will have the best chance possible to grab their part of the American Dream. For that to happen, you have to get the right people in government—people who know when and how to take charge and who also know when to let go. Our forefathers had a saying: Eternal vigilance is the price of liberty. In other words, stay alert, because the bureaucrats are always out there waiting for the chance to confuse the issues and destroy incentives. If we let them, it will be nobody's fault but our own.

One final thought.

Historian Arthur M. Schlesinger Jr., in *The Cycles of American History*, has popularized the idea that there are cycles in American history (an idea that originated with his father, another famous historian). Schlesinger said that government activism appears in cycles. Every twenty years or so, Americans get interested in activist government. We give our hearts and minds to a Franklin Roosevelt and his New Deal, then a generation later to a John F. Kennedy and his New Frontier.

The converse, Schlesinger wrote, is also true. Every twenty years or so, as a nation we retreat back into ourselves. He portrays the Eisenhower years and the Reagan years as times of thoughtless, insular selfishness. He uses terms that make the American people during these periods sound both selfish and sleepy.

"These are times of 'privatization,' (barbarous but useful word), of materialism, hedonism, and the overriding quest for personal gratification," Schlesinger writes.

I'm not a professional historian, let alone a distinguished historian. I'm a guy who knows how to put big deals together. I know how to get the work done on time and under budget. And when I think about what I see in my work, day in and day out, it strikes me that Schlesinger has it only half right.

I get a warm feeling when I remember the idealism of the Kennedys. I'd like to see that spirit rekindled in Washington.

But let's not kid ourselves. The American people never go to sleep. We're like New York or New Orleans or every interstate in the country at three o'clock in the morning. Someone's always awake. Someone's always busy creating something new and astonishing. I find it more than a little insulting, frankly, that an educated person would believe that because Washington, D.C., is relatively peaceful the spirit of activism is somehow asleep in this country.

The Eisenhower years, the Reagan years were periods of strong cultural and economic activity. The same has been true even during this Age of Clinton.

I don't accept the notion that the creative activities going on at times like these are not valid because they don't bear the stamp of some government program presided over by a sugar-daddy president.

What have we been doing? Americans have been busy making movies. Opening dry cleaners, health clubs, and restaurants. Building airplanes. Creating the computer revolution.

Some, I know, will dismiss these words. They'll object, saying: A dry cleaners? You've got to be kidding me. Restaurants? Health clubs? What do you call this, Trump? Strip-mall activism? I don't mind the term at all.

To such critics I say: When was the last time the air force flew you to a nice beach vacation? Or the Department of Health and Human Services cleaned your clothes or fed you lunch? Or the government made a movie worth watching?

The business of America truly is business, because business is the task of linking private ambitions to social needs. The couple that opens the dry cleaners or runs the corner restaurant does so in pursuit of their personal version of the American Dream. The rest of us need to get our clothes cleaned. We need to eat. We all want to travel, to be entertained, to have a good job and get ahead.

So far, no one has been able to do a better job of providing for these community needs than the men and women of American business. And American business is not only conglomerates. It is also the handiwork of the American people. The triumph of American business embodies the very spirit of millions of American entrepreneurs.

Only a professor could believe that the unleashed creative genius of the American people isn't activism.

I say business and work are the featured events of our history—the real story of America. It's what happens at city hall or in the Rose Garden of the White House that's the sideshow.

We need to keep this truth firmly in mind should we actually face the economic decline that I think may be in our future.

First, reduction of regulation will put more money in the hands of more people. It will raise all boats.

Second, the possible negative effects of international trade or the actions of the major players, from megacorporations to the Counsel of Economic Advisors, will be buffered by healthy local economies.

Third, there's a lesson to be learned from the tragic reports from the one-time Soviet Union. Communism has fallen, the party is no longer in control, the citizens of the Soviet states have an opportunity for the first time in generations to take charge of their own lives and to build a Western-style free-market democracy. With the size of their workforce and the abundance of their natural resources, these states could be major economic players. But the stories coming out of Russia and other countries today are horrifying. Graft is everywhere, the currency is plummeting, the mob controls a huge amount of economic power, lines of communication are down. Everywhere you turn there is lying, corruption, and chaos. The problem is easy to analyze. Soviet citizens never learned how to work. They never were given a chance to see the connection between effort and reward. They still don't understand anything about self-interest or self-motivation. The worker on endless break at Wollman Rink before I took the job over was a small model of most Russian workers. He's a contagion that must be eradicated from the American system.

★   ★   ★

I'm going to sound like somebody's Dutch uncle here, but I think it's obvious that a healthy economy puts everybody who contributes to the economy into fighting trim. A well-trained, positive-thinking, energetic workforce will get us out of whatever may be coming.

And maybe it's time to start handicapping your local economist and politicians.

CHAPTER TWO

Competition: Saving Our Schools the American Way

IT'S UNACCEPTABLE. OUR SCHOOLS AREN'T centers of learning, they're centers of crime. Do you think your kid is safe if he or she is off the streets? Do you imagine orderly classrooms?

In 1997–98, 28,534 incidents were reported. . . . The total number of reported incidents in 1997–98 was 30 percent higher than in 1996–97, when 21,993 incidents were reported. . . . 1,966 Level 1 offenses—the most serious level of incident—were reported. . . . Level 1 offenses include "offenses against people," such as robbery with or without a weapon, assault with or without a weapon, sex offenses, kidnapping, and homicide; and "offenses against property," such as grand larceny, burglary, and arson. . . . 9,175 Level 2 offenses—a middle degree of incident—were reported. . . . Level 2 offenses include "offenses against people," such as menacing, reckless endangerment, and attempted or actual suicide; "offenses against property," such as vandalism and larceny . . . and weapon and drug seizures.

A large share of this increase is accounted for by a vast 47-percent increase in the number of weapon- and drug-seizure incidents: 4,320 in 1997–98, compared to 2,932 in 1996–97. . . . [An additional] 1,556 weapons and prohibited items were seized [by scanning].

No, the above statistics aren't from the police log for the mean streets of East St. Louis; they're from the Board of Education's annual report on school violence and safety in New York City's public schools.

That's right. All those violent incidents involved school kids, on school grounds.

On the bright side, the New York City schools are proud to report that there was not a single homicide all year. And the number of sex offenses was down too—from 126 in 1996–97 to 121 in 1997–98. That's five fewer incidents of "sex abuse and sodomy" in public schools than in 1996–97.

These horrifying numbers are just one sign that something fundamental is wrong with our schools. Hugely wrong. We used to worry about the schoolyard bully giving our kid a bloody nose and stealing his milk money. Now we're worried that our kid will get caught in the crossfire or that our daughters will be sexually assaulted in a stairwell.

Moreover, as the murder spree in Littleton, Colorado, indicates—as if we hadn't already learned from Pearl, Mississippi, or Edinboro, Pennsylvania, or Jonesboro, Arkansas, or West Paducah, Kentucky, or Springfield, Oregon—school violence isn't just a big-city problem anymore. The idea of escaping to the safety of the suburbs completely evaporated in the horror of Littleton. All across America, the story's the same.

Our schools aren't safe, which is bad enough. On top of that, our kids aren't learning. Too many are dropping out of school and into the street life—and too many of those who do graduate are getting diplomas that have been devalued into "certificates of attendance" by a dumbed-down curriculum that asks little of teachers and less of students. Schools are crime-ridden *and* they don't teach. Combine those facts and you're looking at a pretty bleak future for America.

Today's economy may be humming along, but how long do we think the United States can survive schools that pretend to teach while our kids only pretend to learn? How can we hope for a healthy society when kids are being forced into a war-zone mentality before they reach their teens. How can a kid hope to build an American Dream when he hasn't been taught how to spell the word "dream"?

Public education was never meant only to teach the three Rs, history, and science. It was also meant to teach citizenship. At the lower levels it should cover the basics, help students develop study habits, and prepare those who desire higher education for the tough road ahead. It's a mandate the public schools have delivered on since their inception. Until now.

Those of us whose school years are far behind us like to think back and say, "Our schools used to do a better job."

Well, guess what? They did. What's happening today? *Newsday* reports this about New York City:

- More than half of all New York City public school students in third through eighth grade are reading below grade level.

- Just 48.4 percent of all kids who entered ninth grade in the fall of 1993 graduated with their class in the spring of 1997.

- When the City University of New York voted to end its remedial programs it was estimated that as many as 46 percent of its applicants would be unable to pass the basic entrance exams.

It isn't only in New York City that good schools have gone bad. Widen the lens and the picture is the same.

In the United States, 38 percent of all fourth graders are reading below a "basic" level. Only 24 percent of fourth graders read at a proficient level. Only 7 percent read at an advanced level. The *Milwaukee Journal Sentinel* reports that approximately 70 percent of fourth graders read below what is considered a "proficient" level.

According to a nationwide study by the Thomas B. Fordham Foundation, the percentage of U.S. college kids taking remedial classes is 30 percent. In other words, about a third of our students are going to college to learn what they should have learned in high school. Parents and taxpayers are paying once in high school, once in college to educate kids in the basics. They're getting fleeced. Nor is remedial education going to save us.

We're doing worse than treading water; we're going under. According to school-testing experts' rule of thumb, the average child's achievement score *declines* about 1 percent for each year they're in school. That gives the expression "dumbing down" a whole new meaning. Schools may be hazardous to your child's intellectual health.

What happened to our schools—and how can we fix them?

We can start by learning what's wrong.

2 × 2 = SOMEWHERE BETWEEN 3 AND 6

"Estimating," they call it. When I was in school, they called an answer like that something else: Wrong.

They had a solution: Back to the flash cards.

But the people running our public schools, like people at the upper echelons of a lot of segments in our society, don't want to damage a student's self-esteem. They're concerned about "empowerment." They're worried kids will feel bad if they get a problem wrong or flunk a spelling test. It's better, these people think, to pat a kid on the head and praise his "creative spelling" than point out that there is a traditional name for people with poor spelling skills. We call them illiterates.

Some educators—and educational administrators, who are at the heart of the problem—think being "judgmental" is the worst of all sins. The problem is that life tends to judge—and harshly at that. There's no room for mathematical error when you're setting the dials on a chemotherapy machine. Or launching a space shuttle. Or mixing concrete for the foundation of Trump Tower, for that matter. Try giving a number "in the neighborhood of" on your tax returns and you may end up in a place where there's a very definite number stamped on the back of your shirt.

There's no question that schools are teaching math badly, with devastating effects on students. Here are some of the hard numbers on U.S. student achievement:

In the 1998 Third International Math and Science Study (TIMSS), U.S. twelfth graders ranked nineteenth out of twenty-one nations in math and sixteenth out of twenty-one in science.

In 1983 the U.S. Department of Education published "A Nation at Risk," the study that put the education crisis in the spotlight. Here's the bad news from the Fordham Foundation: Since 1983, U.S. schools have graduated twenty million American twelfth graders who can't do basic math, and twenty-five million who don't know the basics of American history. Over that same period, six million Americans dropped out of high school altogether.

The study goes on to say:

> The numbers are even bleaker in minority communities. In 1996, 13 percent of all blacks aged sixteen to twenty-four were not in school and did not hold a diploma. 17 percent of first generation Hispanics had dropped out of high school, including a tragic 44 percent of Hispanic immigrants in this age group.

The report calls these kids "another lost generation."

Some people like to call this a tragedy. Yet a tragedy, in the traditional sense, is brought on by a fatal personal flaw. The musical genius who destroys himself with alcohol is a tragic figure. Our school debacle, however, is the result of very deliberate, very misguided policies. And it will only be resolved by very deliberate action on the part of ordinary Americans who say they've had enough!

THE LOST ART OF READING

If reading were gone, some would say, we'd enter a new Dark Ages. My vision is even more frightening. I think there'd still be the flickering lights from the TV screens. Not long ago, I read a couple of news articles—a kind of newsprint food-fight, really—about who could take credit for a small increase in national reading scores for fourth graders. Reading scores improved by about 1.3 percent from 1994 to 1998. Usually the press conference at which the annual scores are announced attracts reporters who cover the education beat, and no one else. But not this year. This time Vice President Gore showed up to take center stage to crow about the improvement in reading scores. Gore failed to note that this rise simply brought reading scores back to their 1992 levels.

I reacted to Gore's education strut in a way that any Mets or Cubs or Red Sox fan would understand. I was a Mets fan from the beginning. Not the glory days when the Amazin' Mets shot from last to first in 1969, but back before that, in the days when Marv Throneberry played first and the Mets finished last, in the National League basement, year after year.

What do the Mets have to do with reading scores? Back when the Mets were doormats, we celebrated when they won two games in a row. But when you're thirty-nine games behind the league leader, two straight wins don't get you out of tenth place. Nobody was fooled. We loved the Mets, but despite their "streak" we knew they were still losers.

So when the president and vice president want to break out the bubbly and claim credit for a small uptick in test scores, I'm glad for small favors. But the guys claiming credit still sound like losers. Hearing about school improvement is like hearing someone brag that their kid was arrested on three felonies instead of four. The kid's still in jail, folks. If the celebrants want praise, are they ready to shoulder all blame for declining scores since the day they took office? And is there really anywhere for U.S. scores to go—but up?

Memo to President Clinton and Vice President Gore: Get serious.

MONEY AND SCHOOLING

Ask the people who run our public schools what's the matter, and they say it's simple: There's not enough money.

That's the one-size-fits-all remedy for whatever's ailing us educationally in this country, at least as far as the educrats are concerned. "Our cash-starved public schools"—I've read and heard the phrase so many times, I half expect to see it chiseled in stone over the school door: Cash-Starved Lincoln Middle School.

What they're telling us is this: If you paid us more, we would do the job that is expected of us.

Could it be true we're not spending enough on education? Let's look at the numbers (most of these come from the NCES, the National Center for Educational Statistics, a federal agency):

In current dollars—adjusted for inflation—overall spending on elementary and secondary education in U.S. public schools rocketed from $15.6 billion in 1961 to $293 billion in 1997. Factoring out inflation, that's over a 200 percent increase in just one generation's time.

Over that same period, per-pupil spending almost tripled—from $2,477 to $6,961. Again, that's in today's dollars, after adjusting for inflation.

What did we get for all that money? We increased the size of the teacher force by 1.9 million from 1960 to 1997. We've driven down the pupil-teacher ratio—President Clinton's new scapegoat for slumping scores. It was 25.8 to 1 in 1960 and fell to 17.2 to 1 in 1998. Even in urban public schools, where overcrowded classrooms are supposed to be the norm, the pupil-teacher ratio is 18.5 to 1—less than a student and a half higher than the national average.

Over that same thirty-seven-year span, we raised public-school teacher salaries 32 percent, after inflation. If you teach in an urban public school, according to the American Federation of Teachers, you're likely to earn about 11 percent *more* than the average public school teacher nationwide. This is being tightfisted? I don't think so.

Here's a painful irony about the surge in public school spending. The national average may be $6,146 per pupil, but some of our biggest public school districts (which have the biggest problems) spend a good bit more than that. New York City public schools spent $7,617 in 1998. Across the river in Newark it was $10,925. In Washington, D.C., they spent $8,290. In Boston, $8,225.

More spending per pupil, smaller class sizes, better-paid teachers—all of that must have resulted in better educational performance, right?

Wrong. Incredibly wrong. From the mid-1960s to 1991, SAT scores dropped like an anvil, an average of sixty-two points.

That should have set off some major alarm bells. How can we be living in a time of prosperity, spending like mad on education, trying every innovation our specialists trotted out—and still scores keep dropping?

In fact in 1995 our kids were finishing behind Japan in both math and science, despite the fact that Japan spends much less per pupil.

Did we demand an accounting from our schools of where the money went? Did heads roll, given the outpouring of resources and the lack of results? Did we sound the alarm for real education reform?

No, no, and no. Instead we allowed experts to "re-center" the SAT—which means jiggering the average to reflect our new, lower set of scores. There's a better word for re-centering, one that captures what is really at work here: fraud.

Some students may like getting higher scores for no better performance. That's like getting a raise even though you don't deserve one. In real-world terms they have been seriously misled. They have been told that they are better educated than they are. They believe they are prepared to move up the educational or job ladder.

Wrong.

The education industry is delivering less for more money and claiming no ground has been lost. It's fraud, pure and simple.

The question we've got to ask ourselves is: What are we getting for all that investment?

A. not enough educational achievement

B. too much double-talk from the educrats

C. a bigger school bureaucracy

D. all of the above

The correct answer is D—which, come to think of it, is about the grade U.S. schools deserve.

As I mentioned earlier, there's another issue here as well. Are we spending our money the right way? Might it be, as Richard Kahan suggests, that we ought to invest in the physical plant rather than in educational bureaucracy and teachers' salaries? It's worth considering. It's clear we're not spending correctly now.

As much as it pains me to admit the limitations of wealth, add educational achievement to the things money can't buy. Study after study has found absolutely no correlation between education spending and educational achievement. Eric Hanushek, another school researcher, comes to a similar conclusion. In other words, plenty of states that spent less per pupil showed levels of educational achievement higher than states that spent more.

That's an awful lot of time and effort to prove something we should have known all along: Whether we're talking about investing in education or anything else, what we get in return is never just a matter of how much we spend, but how well.

SELF-ESTEEM, SELF-WORTH, AND SELF-RESPECT

One major problem is the educators' chief objective: building self-esteem.

The 1991 International Assessment of Educational Progress ranked U.S. students twelfth out of fourteen in international math achievement. According to Daniel McGroarty, a school-choice advocate, that same study also surveyed kids from each nation on how they *felt* about their math ability. Ninety percent of the U.S. kids polled reported a "positive attitude" about math. South Korean kids—the ones who finished first in math achievement—had the least positive attitude toward their math abilities.

There it is: You've got a South Korean kid doing calculus in junior high and worrying that he doesn't have what it takes. Meanwhile,

American kids may add two plus two and get five, but they're encouraged to feel damn good about themselves. Their teachers probably even gave them smiley-face stickers to celebrate the achievement.

This kind of feel-good nonsense has taken over our schools. It's apparently never too early to start feeding egos. *Education Week* writes about a New Jersey program for kids as young as kindergarten age. The program is called "I Like Me!" The *Los Angeles Times* reports that at Loren Miller Elementary School in Los Angeles, kids spent a part of each day doing "I Love Me" lessons—all the more impressive when you consider that, at the time, their average test scores barely registered in the low double-digits. Nationwide there have been more than ten thousand research studies looking for a connection between high self-esteem and lower levels of crime, drug abuse, or better educational achievement. They haven't found a connection yet, and I bet they won't.

Our kids are smarter than we give them credit for—especially when it comes to sniffing out hypocrisy. We pump them full of self-esteem, tell them they're great when their schoolwork and school effort tell them otherwise, and they get the message that school is just another con game. How can we expect to raise kids' self-esteem when we lower our expectations?

What's to blame for the failure in education? One popular explanation—at least with the education establishment—is this: The kids are unteachable. (Why change the system when you can blame the students?) After all, they say, take a look at the kids sitting in our classrooms these days, especially in urban schools. Tough cases, right? It's a blackboard jungle in there. That's the not-so-subtle subtext of so many educrats' sob stories about how hard it is to teach the urban school student. Too many one-parent families, too little parental supervision, too little discipline in the home, a lot of sociobabble about the inevitable educational impact of inadequate disposable income—you name it. It all adds up to the party line that some children just can't be educated, no matter how good the school or talented the teacher.

Fortunately, there are a few signs that common sense may be making a comeback. In Bessemer School in Pueblo, Colorado, parents and citizens took action when test scores came back showing just 12 percent of the school's fourth graders reading at grade level. Educators scrapped the school's three-hour-per-week self-esteem sessions and hit the books.

The result: A year later, 64 percent of the kids passed their reading proficiency tests.

It's very easy to make fun of the feel-good educators. I disagree with them; I think being judgmental is exactly what teachers should do. But the truth is that I'm also in favor of building self-esteem. Self-esteem is a personal quality that can help anybody through life. What I oppose is building false self-esteem. It's the definition of the term that's all wrong. Kids are human. They're hungry to succeed. Teachers betray students when they tell them that mediocrity is success.

I say we've got to be firm. Social promotion? Forget it. To tell these kids they get a free pass is the worst thing you can do for them. Michael Jordan, remember, was cut from his high school basketball team. It made him work harder.

Taking high school education seriously means that it is not enough for a youngster to be on the high school rolls and show up occasionally. Dropout prevention is not an end in itself; a youngster who does not pay attention in class and who does not do homework *ought* to drop out. The policy in every high school, including the inner-city high schools with traditionally high dropout rates, should be that students have to be studious in order to receive the public subsidy involved in a high school education.

If we're going to be serious about keeping these kids in line, we have to get rid of the idea that urban kids can't compete and that they can't be required to walk a straight line in school. As an adult I've learned the benefit of running a tight ship. As Lawrence W. Sherman said in the *Wall Street Journal*, "Making schools more firm and consistent in overall discipline works better than D.A.R.E. [an antidrug program]." He added that tougher strategies "lack political advocates and lose out in the competition for funding."

What stands in the way of the reform we all know is needed? It's the balance of power: Teachers' unions with too much power; parents with too little—less and less power, the lower down the economic income ladder you go.

Start with the teachers' unions. The National Education Association and the American Federation of Teachers might think they're different from other unions—they may even call themselves professional associations to show they're a cut above. But just because you've got chalk dust on your sleeve instead of drywall dust on your dungarees doesn't change things. Unions are unions. That's something I know all about. They help workers in the construction trades but not in education.

All in all, it's probably more refreshing to deal with the Teamsters than the AFT or NEA. At least the leaders of the

Teamsters don't blow smoke about professional this and academic that.

The construction unions I deal with want more in the pay envelope for their rank and file. That's what they push for, that's what they tell you the first time you meet and every time you sit down at the table, morning to midnight. You can respect that—even as you push back to cut the best deal from your perspective. That's the American way.

People may sing songs of praise to the competition that makes capitalism what it is, but what we all want is monopoly—dominance in our chosen line of work that allows us to call the tune. No one really *wants* to compete—they *have to* in order to survive. Everyone pursues monopoly, the system prevents it, and the result is the world's most competition-intensive economy.

Who wins?

Consumers do. They get more choice and more quality at lower cost.

SCHOOL SHOPPING

If you really want to see how school choice will strengthen both public and private schools and give our kids better education options, you don't need to conduct a comparative tour of inner-city classrooms. Just come with me to the corner market.

Everyone knows that two bodegas on the block are better than one—as long as the same family doesn't own both, of course. Why is that? Because two or more supermarkets on the same city block means competition—fresh produce, reasonable prices, specials aimed at attracting customers who have other places they can shop.

Find me a market that has the block to itself. Go on in, tell the grocer you've got a problem with the freshness of his produce, and see what happens. You might think the lettuce is a little limp and brown around the edges, but how many blocks are you going to drag your shopping cart to find something fresher?

You're locked in—and the level of service you get, or the lack of it, reflects that.

The same holds true for schools. Our public schools have grown up in a competition-free zone, surrounded by a very high union wall.

Why aren't we shocked at the results? After all, teachers' unions are motivated by the same desires that move the rest of us. And they know how to play the political game. With more than 85 percent of their soft-money donations going to Democrats—and with one out of eight delegates at the 1996 Democratic National Convention a member of the NEA or AFT—teachers' unions know they can count on the politicians they back to take a strong stand against school choice. If not, they'll find candidates who will.

Our public schools are capable of providing a far more competitive product than they do today. Look at some of the high school tests from earlier in this century and you'll wonder if they weren't college-level tests. Many college graduates—and I'm including myself—would be hard pressed to do well on some of these.

It's a straightforward clash of issues:

The Brotherhood of Blackboard Workers wants to keep the door closed to competition. That way they can run things as they choose, without review.

And we've got to bring on the competition—open the school-house doors and let parents choose the best school for their children.

Education reformers call this school choice, charter schools, vouchers, even opportunity scholarships.

I call it competition—the American way.

What will make our schools work harder? Give students and parents a choice as to where to send their kids. After all, if that school doesn't do right by their child, they're right back out in the market again, looking for a school that suits them better. And in an environment where there's competition and choice, there's a constant effort to offer quality at competitive cost.

Sound familiar?

That's why guys like businessmen Teddy Forstmann and John Walton are trying to jump-start school reform by underwriting $100 million in voucher "scholarships" for more than 50,000 kids nation-wide. They know business. They know the power of competition to improve things and they know the quality of workmanship when monopoly prevails: low quality for high prices.

That's why school choice caught on in Milwaukee and Cleveland—the only two cities today where parents (in this instance, low-income families) can direct their share of state-provided educa-tion funding to follow their child to the school of their choice. That's why Mayor Giuliani wants to see New York introduce school choice as a catalyst for change. As the mayor put it, "We should not be afraid to basically turn the evaluation of schools over to the consumers, the parents and the children."

That's why private philanthropists have started programs in forty more American cities to do what public policy hasn't done: broaden education options to thousands more kids. That's why thirty-four states have adopted charter school laws that give individual groups of teachers, local businesses, universities, and nonprofit groups the right to use public funds to open schools of their own with new curriculums and special programs to succeed with students where others have failed.

What will public school officials do if they're confronted with school-choice programs? Will they compete to see which system can offer the best education to kids?

They'll sue.

That's what the public education establishment did in Milwaukee, where the country's first-ever school-choice program was established in 1990. The teachers' unions' lobbyists fought tooth and nail to keep the program from getting through the Wisconsin legislature. When the lobbyists lost, the lawyers came in—and sued to stop a thousand low-income Milwaukee parents from claiming the school-choice voucher the state had voted to give them.

That's not all. The state superintendent who wanted to kill the school-choice program picked a school-choice skeptic to conduct the annual official review, in hopes they'd be able to study the program to death. And each year those studies came out—a steady drizzle of hyped-up negative findings on a program parents saw as a ray of sunshine for their kids.

But Milwaukee parents fought all the way up to the U.S. Supreme Court, which let the decision stand. The Milwaukee program survived, and today provides vouchers to 15,000 children from low-income families across the city, says Daniel McGroarty in *Break These*

Chains. The public school establishment tried to kill school choice in Milwaukee. So far they've failed.

There's another argument that needs debunking. Defenders of the status quo insist, usually at the top of their lungs, that parental choice means the end of public schools.

Let's look at the facts.

Right now, nationwide, nine out of ten children attend public schools. If you look at public education as a business—and with nearly $300 billion spent each year on K-through-twelve education in the United States, it's a very big business indeed—it would set off every antitrust alarm bell at the Department of Justice and the Federal Trade Commission.

When teachers' unions say even the most minuscule program allowing school choice is a mortal threat, they're saying: If we aren't allowed to keep 90 percent of the market, we can't survive.

When Bell Telephone had 90 percent of the market, a federal judge broke it up.

Who's better off? The kids who use vouchers to go to the school of their choice, or the ones who choose to stay in public school?

All of them.

That's the way it works in a competitive system.

In the courts, in the state legislatures, in cities across the country—and, as I write this chapter, finally on the state level as well—school choice is gaining ground. In April 1999, Jeb Bush and the Florida legislature passed an education reform bill, including a provision that makes "opportunity scholarships" in the amount of $4,000 available to kids whose public schools rate a failing grade in terms of achievement-test scores.

Good policy. Even smarter politics. By giving choice to kids trapped in Florida's failing public schools, Jeb Bush is forcing public-education apologists to admit they hate vouchers so much they'd keep kids locked into even the worst public schools before they'd give them a choice and a chance. It all reminds me of events back in the South a few short decades ago. Instead of integrating, schools in Virginia shut down. It was called "massive resistance" and it was a stain on this country's honor, a moral scandal. And so is keeping low-income kids in schools that all but guarantee failure.

When it comes to the best educational environment for any individual kid, there's no one-size-fits-all answer. It might be the public school down the street or the magnet school across town. It could be a religious or military academy.

The right school will enable a child to blossom. Parents know that instinctively, no matter what politicians say. Look at President Clinton and Vice President Gore—those tireless opponents of school choice. What do they do, not as politicians but as parents, when the time comes to send their own children to school? For Chelsea Clinton, the choice was Sidwell Friends, one of the most expensive, exclusive prep schools anywhere in the United States. For Al Gore, the choice was even simpler: for his son, his own alma mater, St. Albans; for his daughters, National Cathedral School.

A couple of years ago, when he celebrated his fiftieth birthday, President Clinton saluted the teacher who made the biggest difference in his life. She was Sister Mary Amaia McGee, a Catholic nun who was Bill Clinton's second-grade teacher at St. John's School in Hot Springs, Arkansas.

According to *Newsday*, President Clinton's mother, Virginia Kelley, remembered it this way: "I recognized that Bill was very special and I wanted him in a good school."

President Clinton, your mama was right.

Shouldn't every mother and father in every city across America have the right to send their child to the school that's special for them? All of us—except the union-captivated politicians—know the answer to that question.

DISCIPLINE AND SELF-DISCIPLINE

To achieve higher standards, students need discipline. And the failure to teach discipline is where the schools break down. I'd bet that it's one of the first things most parents look for in choosing a school.

I learned about discipline when I was a teenager. When I was eleven and twelve I was cocky, full of myself, beginning to be full of unfamiliar hormones. My father saw what was coming and headed me off in time. He put me in a military school in Croton-on-Hudson for four years. It was one of the most difficult and valuable periods of my life. My father taught himself discipline. Or he learned it from life, losing his own father and having to take care of his family. I had to learn discipline from others so that I could later impose it on myself.

Meanwhile, pity the poor public school teacher, who can't enforce rules. If he or she can't teach these kids, who will?

Brother Louis, that's who.

He's the Capuchin friar who's principal of Our Lady Queen of Angels in East Harlem. Amity Schlaes wrote about him in the *Wall Street Journal* in an article that stands out in my memory.

Walk into the third-grade class at Our Lady and listen to the children read aloud—70 percent at or above grade level. Walk down the street to PS 102, where just one in five third-graders read at grade level, and Our Lady's achievement grows even more impressive.

Both schools happen to be in one of the poorest neighborhoods in America and both schools draw kids from the same hard world. Kids from one-parent families? Our Lady has them. Overcrowded classrooms? Our Lady has those too; the eighth-grade class has forty-six kids. Most of them will go on to Catholic high schools—where 98 percent of the students graduate in four years.

There is one difference, of course, between Our Lady and the typical public school—a difference that means all the world. If PS 102's kids underperform, their poor test scores will just become another talking point in the push for more school funding. If Brother Louis doesn't do his job and the quality of education slips, there *won't be any* Our Lady, because the parents who enroll their children there are paying customers, free to take their kids somewhere else. Families are involved. Brother Louis and his faculty are teaching in the free market. They can't afford slipping test scores. They dig in and make kids learn, whatever it takes. What's the key? Our Lady's handbook says, "Self-discipline is the Christian ideal which all students are encouraged to achieve." Students who aren't making the grade are suspended.

How much does it cost to enroll a child at Our Lady? $1,585 a year. A far cry from the $7,617-per-student spent by New York City public schools.

Still, in a private school, tuition doesn't always tell the whole story. Endowments and annual donations help meet educational expenses while keeping tuition costs low. All told, tuition included, Our Lady Queen of Angels spends about $2,500 a year to educate each student. Follow the trajectory from grade school to high school: Our Lady produces twice as many graduates, at half the cost for each.

But what about the downside we've heard about parochial education? Critics say that private schools are exclusive—and exclusionary—while public schools are the melting pot. The fact is, the average urban Catholic school today has a more diverse mix of students—more African American and Asian and Hispanic and White kids sitting side by side—than schools in cities and school districts where they've spent billions of dollars to bus kids an hour away from their neighborhoods for the right racial mix. They've got a sizable percentage of kids who aren't even Catholic and have no desire to become so—sent there not because there are crucifixes in the classrooms, but because their parents see parochial school as the best place for them to learn, period. They prefer an educational catechism that says two plus two still equals four, and cat isn't spelled with a "k."

A ghetto public school, Chicago Military Academy–Bronzeville, is experimenting with a new kind of classroom order. Students wear uniforms. If they act up in class they do pushups. The academy is recruiting students for the armed forces. It's an experiment in teaching real discipline to kids who are going to face a struggle. It aims to give them the tools they need to get out into the world and to have a chance. Parents and students love it.

I'm not suggesting the magic bullet for education has to be a religious or a military academy. It could be an independent community school with no religious affiliation at all. It could be a school that has a partnership with a business.

But don't expect public schools to compete when they've got a captive audience. That's not human nature.

If you want to get involved in education reform, you don't have to have be a congressman or a Wall Street wizard or have the keys to the Trump Tower in your pocket. Just ask Luis Iza Jr., a Cuban-born diamond broker in Midtown Manhattan, who was written up in the *Washington Post*.

Iza helps rescue poor kids from failing schools in his old Washington Heights neighborhood, a mix of Dominican immigrants and second-generation families from Cuba and Puerto Rico. Iza's not backed by a big bureaucracy operating out of prime Park Avenue space; he runs the whole thing out of a couple of file folders in a broom closet of a room at the back of his own office.

It all started one Sunday afternoon as he walked down the church steps after mass in his old neighborhood. A mother came up to him with tears in her eyes, telling Iza that she was worried her son would get involved with a gang if she didn't get him out of his public school. All she knew was that Iza had survived Washington Heights and made a success of himself. She was begging for help. Iza promised he would.

That was twelve years ago. Iza helped that woman's son, and word spread. Today Luis Iza's Operation Exodus has placed over two hundred kids in schools ranging from preschools in Manhattan to boarding schools in Texas. Operation Exodus provides after-school programs, mentoring programs, and summer schools. Iza does it by partnering with schools that can provide 75 percent of their tuition in the form of scholarships. Operation Exodus and the student's family then collaborate to pay off the remaining 25 percent. The families themselves—many of them living at or under the poverty level—gladly find a way to kick in $500 to $2,000 a year to give their children a better chance at life. Of the one hundred high school students currently enrolled in Operation Exodus, all are currently planning to attend college and have cumulative SAT scores that are almost 400 points higher than the local Washington Heights high schools. All of Operation Exodus's past high school graduates went on to college. A better chance at life, indeed.

There's no better way I know to boost a kid to a brighter future. And no place where education matters more, or opens more doors, than it does right here in America. I've made it clear that our system is in crisis, but I hope I've made it equally clear that there is plenty of reason to hope. We know our kids can achieve—no matter what their background. We also know what we can do to help them achieve, and who is standing in the way of improvement.

And equally important, we know that politicians follow the winds of public opinion, which is why it's important for all of us to stand up for real school reform. That will mean different things for different people. The only non-option is inaction.

What's missing from the education debate? A sense of urgency. Even the crusaders don't realize that time is running out. Listen to Rudy Crew, chancellor of the New York City school system:

We don't have a lot of time, which is why I feel this incredible urgency [for reform]. I think we have ten years, tops, to turn the [public school] system around before the public gets fed up and begins to replace it with something else.

Now, Rudy Crew is a smart and decent man who wants to do right by our kids. But with all due respect, parents with children in under-performing schools today can't wait ten years to see if things get better. In ten years, the six-year-old who doesn't know his alphabet today is the sixteen-year-old statistic—another dropout, another kid who forfeits his future because the schools failed him. Rudy Crew is right. We should all feel a sense of urgency. But we don't have ten years to turn things around. We've got to do it now.

My friend Floyd Flake knows that. That's why, as an African American congressman representing his Queens neighborhood, he bucked the Democratic establishment and became a strong school-choice supporter:

> . . . This issue transcends party. This issue transcends race. It deals with a simple question of educating our young people. . . . The [public] school system is not doing that. There are too many children who are stuck, too many children who have lost their dreams, have lost their hope of ever being able to be competitive in the society in which we live.

Nobody's more locked into underperforming public schools than poor kids and their families. And let's call this idea, that poor urban parents aren't capable of making good educational choices for their children, what it is: racism. These parents worry for their kids as much as families in Shaker Heights or Beverly Hills—and probably more so.

I don't mean to say that all educators are corrupt or stupid. There are plenty of hardworking people with useful, innovative ideas who should be heard.

So, by all means, lengthen the class day. Computerize the classroom—or return to the three Rs. Raise standards, remove regulations, create a school without walls—or make kids wear uniforms in the classroom. Let all of these education experiments unfold, just so long as we let parents choose the programs they believe to be best for their kids. Competition will do the rest.

★   ★   ★

Let's review how I'd save our schools and best serve the students we're depriving of a first-class education.

- Start by giving all parents a choice as to where they send their kids to school. Then challenge all our schools, public as well as private, to ask more of their teachers and more of their students. We'll see our schools improve.

- Demand competition and choice—that's the American way. It's the way out of the education mess we're in and the way forward to the well-educated workforce we'll need to make America the envy of the world.

- Know your local candidates. Find out how much they're taking in contributions from the teachers' unions. Make sure they have spelled out exactly what their position is on these issues. Nothing is more important to the future of America than education.

The Safe Streets
We Deserve

CRIME IS THE SYMPTOM. IT'S like a fever. It shows us that our schools need help. It shows us that our society is in trouble. Crime is the biggest scandal of American life. We live in the richest country on earth, we have opportunities that our grandparents never dreamed of, we enjoy peace, and even our poorer citizens are relatively well off—yet we still have an unacceptable crime rate.

Yes, it has dropped recently, but it is still much higher than it should be and there are many reasons to think that early in the next century, because of population growth, it's going to skyrocket. Our politicians and pundits, of course, don't like to bring that up. They're happy-talking the issue. Once again, they seem to believe that if they don't mention the bad stuff, it might go away. They assume the American people will reject them if they dare tell the truth. It's time to shine some light into this fogbank.

Here's the baseline fact: We can have safe streets. We really do know how to keep the criminal element off guard. But unless we stand up for tough anticrime policies, they will be replaced by policies that emphasize criminals' rights over those of ordinary citizens.

Soft criminal sentences are based on the proposition that criminals are the victims of society. A lot of people in high places really do believe that criminals are victims. And they don't like the methods that have proved successful in crime control. As I write this book, there are protests here in my hometown against Mayor Giuliani's tough (and successful) anticrime policies. I count some of my friends among the protesters. But they're singing a siren song. They basically want us to disarm ourselves when we should be preparing for what my favorite crime expert, James Q. Wilson, warns will be an explosion of violent crime. (Wilson's anthology of expert opinions, *Crime,* is must reading for anyone who wants to understand this problem.) Let's look at the basics:

First: The only victim of a violent crime is the person getting shot, stabbed, or raped. The perpetrator is never a victim. He's nothing more than a predator, and there can be no excuses made for killing old ladies, beating old men, or shooting adolescents.

Second: To compare police officers with Nazis is obscene and makes it obvious that there is a profound opposition to strong anti-crime policies.

Third: There is a philosophy in our country that says criminals plunder because they have little or no choice; that they have been forced into crime by poverty, lack of opportunity, or early childhood mistreatment. That's an excuse? Ridiculous!

Fourth: Tough crime policies are the most important form of national defense. Government's number-one job is to ensure domestic tranquillity, and that means tranquilizing the criminal element as much as possible. Aggressive anticrime policies are the best social program, because they allow citizens in all neighborhoods, and especially the tougher ones, to live and work in a safe environment. They also protect children from the predatory mob that brutalizes them at every turn.

Many friends of mine—and let me point out that they are very well-meaning and decent people—are aware that we can keep crime low if we're willing to take the necessary steps. The problem is that they don't like the necessary steps. They don't like building more prisons. They believe, at the bottom of their hearts, that we put too many criminals in jail. It's an embarrassment to them. Nor do they care for hard-edged anticrime policies like we've had here in New York. Yes, these policies have brought crime rates down several notches, but, they argue, the policies have come at the cost of civil liberties. These people are fearful of establishing a police state.

I respect their earnestness; I respect their intelligence. They also want the best America possible, and they have a good and decent vision of our country. They are every bit as patriotic as I am. But I reject their reasoning on crime.

I like to remind these friends that they would be singing a different tune if they didn't have a doorman downstairs, or if they had to walk through tough streets to get to work or to the grocery store. I kid them by saying that they will call the police if someone scowls at their poodle. The fact is, they don't have much to worry about in the first place, but if something does go wrong they'll be the first to say, Where's a cop when you need him? Their problem is that they think too abstractly about crime, largely because they have no first-hand experience with it. Nor do they tend to know people who have to contend with the criminal element. It's easy for them to believe a criminal is just a regular guy who went off the rails, who can be put straight again with enough time and therapy. Even if this person has killed somebody, they think he can be redeemed.

In the election of 1988 we saw a painful demonstration of this dilemma. Governor Mike Dukakis was running for president and was on record opposing the death penalty. During one of the debates he was asked by CNN's Bernard Shaw what he would do if somebody raped his wife, Kitty. I have no doubt that the governor loves his wife and that he has the same feelings we all do, but he stumbled over his philosophical position and came off looking heartless and confused. He definitely *was* confused.

A few years ago my mother was mugged. She'd gone to the bakery to buy a crumb cake, something my father especially enjoyed. On the sidewalk outside, her purse was snatched. It was done in a violent and shocking way. Mom was thrown to the ground on her face. The thief was not only brutal but also stupid. He committed the crime the day he turned twenty-one. He would be tried as an adult.

After similar misfortune many families might react by holing up, just staying at home with the injured family member, and perhaps even seeking grief counseling. And those are all good ideas.

But in my family we believe in going the extra mile. My brother Robert, who works in Queens, contacted the judge trying the thief. He made a point of being in the courtroom during the trial, so the family presence would be felt. The Trumps believe in getting even.

It's our duty to keep demanding that our public officials hold the line on crime.

WILL THE REAL UNDERDOG PLEASE STAND UP?

Before we get deeper into crime, prisons, and punishment, I want to say one more thing about the people who worry about the plight of criminals. They profess to be concerned for the underdogs. But if they thought things through, they would make all the public officials who are tough on crime their biggest heroes. Nobody—and I repeat, nobody—does more to help the little guy realize his dream than the public official who makes safe streets the top priority.

Criminals target a small percentage of the poor. A recent study shows that most of the violent crime in society occurs in 3 percent of neighborhoods. These are often places where people are struggling to raise families, people who could use all the help they can get. If kids in posh neighborhoods started getting gunned down the way kids have been in the harder sections of towns, my friends would change their tune.

This country was made great by the idea that when a fellow citizen is in need, you don't turn your back. You find a solution. Nobody deserves to fear for their lives, or their children's lives, just because they live in a certain neighborhood. No kid's life should be in jeopardy because he was born to a single mother in a housing project.

When my sister was a single mother, my brother Robert and I made it our business to visit her son, David, almost every afternoon. We'd hang out or play catch; he needed men around to connect with. He's since become a successful clinical neuropsychologist.

The fear of crime makes the problem even worse. To decrease the possibility of encountering a predator, many Americans avoid going to cities to do business, shop, or spend leisure time. We do this so automatically that we don't even realize it. Criminals have partitioned American communities into safe zones and war zones. Cities should be dynamic centers of culture, the arts, and entertainment. The suburbanite or tourist should feel no fear about heading downtown to enjoy the excitement that urban cultural life offers.

Crime fragments America, separating our population, reducing economic and cultural opportunity, and forcing most of us to live in some degree of fear. That is why we need to pull together to make sure that effective anticrime policies aren't watered down or destroyed. We need to establish a zero-tolerance policy toward anyone who is getting in the way of the safer America we all deserve.

What's the best way for ordinary people to support tough crime policies? We need to get our facts in line. Let's start by recognizing a few basics.

We've heard the good news about how crime rates have dropped. But hold the champagne. As I said before, what government and the press don't like to say is that most serious crime experts believe rates will skyrocket early in 2000 because there will be more adolescent boys around, and adolescent boys are especially dangerous.

A lot of these boys don't have fathers. All they've got is a mother and that mother might well be a teenager herself. As anybody knows, a single mother is going to have a hard time controlling a normal boy, especially when he hits strutting age. She can say, "Son, you stay home tonight and do your math," but he won't hear her.

A government study of crime in America warns that when the population of adolescent males rises early next century, we're going to have wolf packs roaming the streets, and not only downtown. If these kids are anything like those who terrorized urban America in recent years, we're in for a very bad time.

Robert E. Moffit, Edwin Meese III, and Patrick F. Fagen's *Crime: Turning the Tide in America,* from the Heritage Foundation's 1998 *Candidate's Briefing Book,* says that from 1985 to 1993, killings involving fifteen-year-olds went up 207 percent, while arrests of eighteen- to twenty-year-old males jumped 119 percent. Adults, by comparison, were less murderous. The rate at which adults killed other adults was no higher in 1990 than it was in 1980, and in many cities it was a lot lower.

We saw plenty of youth mayhem in New York. At Thomas Jefferson High School in Brooklyn, more than fifty students died between 1989 and 1994, mostly around the school but some inside the school itself. You didn't see many front-page moralists showing up over there to protest that slaughter. They didn't dare venture into the neighborhood and I don't blame them.

PRISONS

A permissive attitude toward criminals makes crime more likely, and this will be especially harmful if the expected increase in violence occurs. I could understand the argument that we have too many people in prison if the police were rounding up innocent people and locking them away. But that's not the case. For the most part, you have to be a longstanding criminal to qualify for jail. This will come as news to our opponents in this debate.

Consider for a minute a column in the *Washington Post* written by a woman named Geneva Overholser, who is a pretty good representative of this position. I'm sure she's a very nice woman, but she's passing along ideas that are plainly wrong.

Geneva wrote an article saying we have an "addiction to imprisonment." Her main gripe was that we imprison too many dope dealers, but that's not all she was upset about:

> It's hard now even to remember back to the '60s, when America's prison population was shrinking. Leaders of both parties then talked of emptying the nation's jails of all but the most dangerous criminals and moving to more humane alternatives. Instead we now have mandatory minimum sentences, "three-strikes" laws and other anticrime measures, increasing both the number of people sent to prison out of all those arrested and the length of time served.

I'm not saying that fine-tuning punishment isn't possible. There are undoubtedly criminals in jail for victimless crimes. And if a state is releasing child molesters to make room for new criminals, there's something wrong.

But with all due respect, people who tend to support that kind of policy, and who call for "humane alternatives," understand that these policies don't directly affect them. Try building a halfway house next door to the Overholser residence and you'll soon see what I mean.

America doesn't use prisons much more than any other civilized nation. In Europe the odds of going to prison are higher for some offenses (rape) than they are here, lower for others (assault or burglary), and about the same for robbery or homicide. Prison sentences are generally longer in the United States for any crime other than murder.

Crime expert James Q. Wilson has some other interesting facts we need to be aware of. Europeans have in fact taken the lead in several types of crime. "All the world is coming to look like America," Wilson says:

> In 1981 the burglary rate in Great Britain was much less than in the United States; within six years the two rates were the same; today, British homes are more likely to be burgled than American ones. In 1980 the rate at which automobiles were stolen was lower in France than in the United States; today, the reverse is true. By 1984 the burglary rate in the Netherlands was nearly twice that in the United States. In Australia and Sweden certain forms of theft are more common than they are here.

The fact that we are ahead in murders is nothing new. According to Wilson, "Big American cities have had more homicides than comparable European ones for almost as long as anyone can find records. New York and Philadelphia have been more murderous than London since the early part of the nineteenth century."

No, the problem isn't that we have too many *people* locked up. It's that we don't have enough *criminals* locked up. Wilson's figures show that dangerous criminals had less chance of getting arrested this decade than they did twenty years earlier. And if they got tossed into a state prison, they served shorter sentences than at any time since the 1940s.

Besides keeping criminals off the streets, prisons are also partly responsible for the decrease in crime.

GUNS

It's often argued that the American murder rate is high because guns are more available here than in other countries. After a tragedy like the massacre at Columbine High School, anyone could feel that it is too easy for Americans to get their hands on weapons. But nobody has a good solution.

This is another issue where you see the extremes of the two existing major parties. Democrats want to confiscate all guns, which is a dumb idea because only the law-abiding citizens would turn in their guns and the bad guys would be the only ones left armed. The Republicans walk the NRA line and refuse even limited restrictions.

I generally oppose gun control, but I support the ban on assault weapons and I also support a slightly longer waiting period to purchase a gun.

With today's Internet technology we should be able to tell within seventy-two hours if a potential gun owner has a record.

CAPITAL PUNISHMENT

Long story short, I don't buy the idea that we can redeem all criminals. Redemption is usually considered the business of higher powers. Nor do I buy the line that capital punishment is uncivilized.

People opposed to capital punishment in this country say our high crime rate is caused by our harsh punishments. They've confused cause with effect. I say that major crimes in this country deserve harsh punishments. We haven't gone far enough.

There is no good reason not to execute heinous criminals. Take for instance the terrible dragging death of James Byrd Jr. in Jasper, Texas. We're all familiar with what happened: Three white goons, for no clear reason, waylaid Byrd, a Black man, as he was coming back from a niece's wedding. They chained him behind a truck and dragged him through a poor residential neighborhood until he finally was dismembered. The Texas jury knew what it had to do. At this writing, one of the perpetrators, John William King, has been sentenced to die by lethal injection and a second is about to be sentenced. My only complaint is that lethal injection is too comfortable a way for these criminals to go.

I totally reject the idea that hanging these sorts of criminals is uncivilized. In fact I believe that letting them live would be totally uncivilized. They've taken an innocent life, so they should have to give theirs in return. That's the very least they can do. They don't deserve to be put into a prison where they can spend their time working out, reading, watching television, earning advanced degrees, filing bogus lawsuits, and even getting married. For this type of person, prison is a social promotion.

Nor do I accept the argument that capital punishment doesn't do any good. I think it is a positive in two senses.

First: Civilized people don't put up with barbaric behavior, such as dragging people to death behind pickup trucks. Would it have been civilized to put Hitler in prison? No—it would have been an outright affront to civilization. The same is true of criminals who prey on innocent men, women, and children. By their acts they have not only rejected civilization but also declared war on it. And I don't care if the victim is a CEO or a floor sweeper. A life is a life, and if you criminally take an innocent life you'd better be prepared to forfeit your own.

James Byrd wasn't famous. He didn't have much money or power. He didn't have a job. So, in purely financial terms, you could say he was a nobody.

But he was a human being and an American citizen. He had family and friends who now miss him. And he had his own version of the dream, no matter how humble it might have been. He was anything but a nobody. Any civilization worthy of the name would treat his murderers the same way they would treat rabid animals.

Second: I can't believe that executing criminals doesn't have a deterrent effect. To point out the extremely obvious, 100 percent of the people who are executed never commit another crime. And it seems self-evident (we can't put numbers to this) that a lot of people who might otherwise commit a capital crime are convinced not to because they know there's a chance they could die for it. Not all crime is irrational.

Young male murderers in their teens and twenties, we are constantly told, are led astray by violent music and violent movies. Fair enough. I believe that people are affected by what they read, see, hear, and experience. Only a fool believes otherwise. So you can't say on one hand that a kid is affected by music and movies and then turn around and say he is absolutely *not* affected when he turns on the evening news and sees that a criminal has gone to the chair for killing a child. Obviously capital punishment isn't going to deter everyone. But how can it not put the fear of death into many would-be killers?

There's no hotter crime issue, at least where I live, than capital punishment.

That's why I was glad when George Pataki came to the governorship of New York promising to restore the death penalty. George took a lot of heat, but he's doing civilization's heavy lifting.

In the general population, a huge percentage of crime victims are kids, especially when it comes to violent crime. Kids between twelve and nineteen are twice as likely to be victims of violent crime as people between twenty-five and thirty-four, and three times more likely than people thirty-five to forty-nine. When you compare kids twelve to nineteen with people sixty-five and older, their violent-crime victimization rate is twenty times higher. Thirteen percent of murder victims are under eighteen; 28 percent are under twenty-three. People eighteen to twenty-two, who are only 7 percent of the population, are 15 percent of murder victims.

If your heart is really in helping our diverse population, instead of merely paying lip service, then your first job is to support tough anticrime measures. If you really want to do something for kids, especially the most vulnerable kids, this is where you can make a huge difference.

But I don't want to make this a minority/majority thing. There's way too much of that in America as it is. Instead let me offer a larger principle: The people who wrote our Constitution were clear in their belief that providing for the public safety is at the top of the responsibilities government has. All of us should feel safe in our homes and on our streets. Safety should be a birthright, like free speech. It is the foundation on which the American Dream is built. This is an idea that should unite all of us, no matter where we come from. When we lose our sense of safety, we lose our birthright.

Ten years ago there was a brutal mugging in Central Park of a young woman jogger—a Wall Street executive—by a gang of young men. The woman's life hung in the balance for some time. Somehow, I began to hear about a great deal of sympathy for the young men. They had been so brutalized by the system, it was said, that they couldn't be held entirely responsible for the crime.

I took a full-page ad in the *New York Times* to object and to state my belief that capital punishment would be the proper way to deal with the young men if the woman died. I was amazed by the number of politicians who called to express sympathy but who refused to take a similar position publicly. They were afraid of offending some of their constituents.

That's the response from today's career politicians.

CELL GROWTH

Criminals are often returned to society because of forgiving judges. This has to stop. A judge who decides unilaterally to reduce sentences can cause immediate damage to a community if he or she releases dangerous criminals from jail. That's why we need to hold judges more accountable, and the best way to make that happen is to elect them. When they hurt us, we need to make sure we can vote them out of the job.

Think what wonders a public vote would work on the career of Norma Shapiro, a district court judge in Pennsylvania who was appointed by President Jimmy Carter. I think Carter has done a lot for the world, but Judge Norma Shapiro was not his most brilliant appointment.

Shapiro once ordered the release of six hundred prisoners, apparently because she thought prisons were getting too crowded. I should add that she ordered the release of six hundred prisoners *per week.* Guess what happened next.

As reported in *Crime: Turning the Tide in America,* the U.S. Senate brought in witnesses in June 1997 to find out the extent of the disaster Judge Shapiro had created. They described a nightmare. One witness told the Senate Judiciary Committee that during one eighteen-month period after Shapiro's jailbreak, the released convicts committed nearly ten thousand crimes, including seventy-nine murders, ninety rapes, and hundreds of other violent crimes. One victim, Daniel Boyle, was a twenty-one-year-old Philadelphia police officer. From 1988 to 1992, 20 percent of thugs arrested for killing cops were out on probation or parole. In my opinion, Judge Shapiro was a willing accessory to all those crimes.

Unfortunately, there are plenty of Shapiros out there, which is one major reason why our streets are full of dangerous convicts. According to the bipartisan group Council on Crime in America, on any given day there are about 1.5 times more convicted violent offenders out on the streets on probation or parole than are behind bars.

Clearly we don't have *too many* people in prison. Quite the contrary.

Meanwhile, the rest of us need to rethink prisons and punishment. The next time you hear someone saying there are too many people in prison, ask them how many thugs they're willing to relocate to their neighborhood. The answer: None.

ENFORCEABLE RESTRAINT

What else can we do to make the streets safer? Obviously you can't force self-restraint on would-be criminals. When individuals or communities can't prevent crime, the balance has to be maintained by law enforcement. If people won't restrain themselves, the cops will have to restrain them.

Can restraint be taught? That's not so easy but it can be done, at least to a degree. Let's look at a few things that seem to be working.

We can start out by making it clear to teenage mothers that they aren't going to get public assistance unless they jump through some pretty small hoops. Some people suggest making them live in group homes or live under some kind of adult supervision. That makes sense. A lot of these girls didn't have fathers or full-time parents of any sort. But there are people—I think we can call them saints—who dedicate their lives to helping kids like this. Whoever they are, and whether they work out of a church, a temple, or some kind of public facility, they deserve all our support.

We're also seeing that a lot of the inner-city adults want to do the best they can by their kids, even though they might have made some mistakes before. Jackson Toby, an expert on crime, tells a story about adult learners that I think is worth repeating, and that we should hope is copied across the nation:

> At Chicago's DuSable High School, an all-Black school close to a notorious public housing project, dropouts regarded by current students as middle-aged hungered for a second chance at a high school education. A thirty-nine-year-old father of six children; a twenty-nine-year-old mother of a fourteen-year-old son who, like his mother, was a freshman at DuSable; and a thirty-nine-year-old mother of five children— all had come to believe that dropping out a decade or two earlier had been a terrible mistake. Some of these adult students were embarrassed to meet their children in the hallways, some of their children were embarrassed to have their parents as schoolmates, and some of the teachers at the high school were initially skeptical about mixing teenagers and adults in classes.

But everyone at DuSable High School agreed that the adult students lent seriousness to the education atmosphere and became role models for younger students.

Political advocates, to no one's surprise, back the same kind of programs that coddle older troublemakers. The *Wall Street Journal* reports, "A University of Southern California study of a crime gang prevention program found that the program was actually keeping the gang together and so perpetrating violent crime," author Lawrence Sherman wrote. "When the program went under, the gang broke up and there were less crimes."

We need to try to teach kids restraint, but let's face facts. Society can do only so much in this area. It can't be everyone's parent. What society can do, however, is make it clear that if you choose to break the law there will be consequences.

In New York City, under Mayor Giuliani, law enforcement has set a standard for the rest of the nation. Our murder rate is at its lowest level since 1967. The incidence of forcible rape in the city is below the national average. In fact violent crime is down so much that Bellevue and Columbia-Presbyterian Hospitals are trying to find new ways to train their trauma surgeons.

The fact is that New York is doing well because the police and courts have adopted a crime-fighting attitude that doesn't care where you came from, only how you behave. It doesn't care what your personal background is—it only cares that you obey the law. When you break faith with the law, it only cares about bringing you to justice. It doesn't care if you don't like the idea of going to jail, because this attitude has it that jail is where criminals belong. In fact our police are out hunting for the types of people who should be in jail. Our force is proactive, not reactive.

This attitude is working wonders for all our citizens and especially for those who had been abandoned by previous feel-good administrations.

What has New York been doing right?

Giuliani's first police commissioner, William Bratton, was the first to see that the job of the police wasn't to sit around waiting to answer 911 calls and hope that the person on the other end of the line was still breathing. It was Bratton who reoriented the police from being reactive to being proactive. He targeted patrols and crime prevention on "hot spots." He insisted on treating minor crimes—subway cheaters and minor vandals—as precursors to more serious crimes and potential signals to others that anything goes.

In other words, the word went out: We're not going to let the little stuff slide. That has made the big difference. Sure, it has brought the moral streakers out for a few afternoons of protest. But as our current police commissioner, Howard Safir, points out, the proof is in the pudding. "I'm not going to be bullied by community activists who say, 'We want feel-good cops.' The bottom line is crime reduction."

★   ★   ★

It's time for the real underdogs—you and me—to get up on our hind legs. We must be the perpetrators in a movement to reclaim our streets and neighborhoods, to be able to breathe freely, knowing our kids are safe. We know we deserve a crime-free America. Whatever my official occupation during the next few years, I'm going to be fighting for this dream.

CHAPTER FOUR

The Foreign Policy
We Deserve

T HERE WAS AN OLD-FASHIONED rule in American politics: Politics stops at the water's edge. It was a good rule in many ways; it meant that however much we disagreed at home, we put on a united front for other countries. It would be irresponsible to break that rule. I'm not going to criticize our foreign policy in general, but there are a few specific problems I want to address.

In the modern world you can't very easily draw up a simple, general foreign policy. I was busy making deals during the last decade of the cold war. I would imagine that for employees of the state and defense departments, the world looked very different then. Foreign policy was a big chess game. There was us, the United States and our close allies, and there was them, the Soviet Union. Everybody else was a bystander. Now the game has changed. We're the only major player. We deal with all the other nations of the world on a case-by-case basis. And a lot of those bystanders don't look so innocent.

I believe that the day of the chess player is over. American foreign policy has to be put in the hands of a dealmaker. Two great dealmakers have served as president—one of them was Franklin Roosevelt, who got us through World War II, and the other was Richard Nixon, who began our dialogue with communist China and forced the Russians to the bargaining table to achieve the first meaningful reductions in nuclear arms. A true dealmaker can keep many balls in the air, weigh the competing interests of other nations, and, above all, constantly put America's best interests first. The true dealmaker knows when to be tough and when to back off. He knows when to bluff and he knows when to threaten, understanding that you threaten only when prepared to carry out the threat. The dealmaker is cunning, secretive, focused, and never settles for less than he wants. It's been a long time since America had a president like that.

Maybe we Americans pump ourselves up too much (though we deserve to boast). We love our country, we're proud of our prosperity and democratic way of life. We think that what's self-evident to us must be self-evident to everyone else too. If other countries or governments oppose or conspire against us, we assume there must be some terrible miscommunication—nothing that a few treaties, trade deals, and summit toasts won't patch over. Even during the cold war our diplomats were constantly falling over themselves to make goodwill offerings at the bargaining table, as if the problem were to convince our adversaries of our pure and noble intentions.

We're flirting with the same kind of mistake now in debating the nuclear nonproliferation treaty. All the major powers may sign such a treaty, but no one will obey it but us. I oppose such agreements for the same reason I oppose gun controls—when weapons are banned, only the outlaws have them.

Americans look into the mirror and see big-hearted citizens of the world's only superpower. We've got a lot to brag about. We protect other nations when they're in trouble. We lead the world in foreign aid. We're everyone's favorite trading partner, we take in refugees and immigrants at a million or so a year, we bail out insolvent governments and prop up weak ones, we mediate intractable disputes. We have standing armies and jetfighter squadrons and fleets the world over— we do it all. A lot of the time we don't even bother to send a bill.

This generosity leads to very poor dealmaking.

Because we are such a kind and generous nation, it's hard for us to believe that some people around the world actually don't like us— that we have enemies dead set against us. We're a little naive some- times, acting as older brother to regimes that are playing us for suckers. In fact playing dumb seems to be the formula our foreign- policy thinkers follow. I'm not saying we need to be hardhearted, but we do need to be a lot more hard-headed, or we can expect big trouble ahead.

I can hear the experts now: Where does Trump, the real estate guy, get off thinking he knows more than we do about the interna- tional scene? Experts are always defensive—and for good reason. They're wrong so often.

A little humility would do these people good. During the cold war, for example, the newspapers and policy journals were full of geopolitical deep thinking explaining why America could never hope to prevail over the Soviet Union. The best we could expect was to "contain" communism, these learned people insisted.

They were, of course, totally wrong—wrong about the most important international development in the last half of this century. In business terms, that would be like predicting that communism would become a great economic engine—which, to no one's surprise, was exactly what some authoritative people told us. In the pages of the venerable journal *Foreign Affairs* one expert wrote that "the Soviet Union is not now, nor will it be during the next decade, in the throes of a true economic crisis, for it boasts enormous unused reserves of political and economic stability." What an extraordinary investment opportunity! Fortunately, few businessmen fell for that analysis.

But because very few politicians were ready for the fall of the Eastern Empire, we had no trade strategy for a dismembered Soviet Union. We weren't ready to address the challenges on the international business scene.

Remember in the late 1980s when all the experts warned how the American economy would soon be eclipsed by the Asian Tigers, and how Japan was going to all but take over the world? Today Japan, not nearly as strong as it was, is in a monumental liquidity crisis, while the rest of the Asian nations are lining up, hat in hand, for IMF bailouts. Their battle cry: Feed us—please! And as late as 1991 there was a great deal of fashionable theorizing about "the end of history." The idea was that with the demise of the Soviet Union and the victory of capitalism we were entering a trouble-free era of peace and guaranteed prosperity. These guys apparently hadn't heard of Islamic fundamentalism, miniaturized weapons, terrorism, or the People's Republic of China.

You know what they say about economists: They will know tomorrow why the things they predicted yesterday didn't happen today. Many of America's experts in foreign policy are no different. They write mostly for their fellow experts and—as with journalists and pundits generally—nobody ever bothers going back to check anyone else's track record.

Add it all up and there's only one conclusion: The experts have a very sorry record as odds-makers.

This isn't to say that I don't study what knowledgeable people have to say. One of the true experts in foreign relations, the great military strategist Karl von Clausewitz, long dead, gave advice I still find valuable: "Know your enemy." Every time our country has come to grief in world affairs it's been because we didn't pay attention. Whenever we think we're invulnerable, whenever we look around the world and start to feel all safe and sound, as if it's all smooth sailing up ahead and the world is full of friends, that's when the icebergs start appearing just off the bow. *Titanic* was a great movie, but the decision-making skills of the great ship's captain are a terrible model for how to conduct foreign policy.

HARD-HAT DIPLOMACY

Henry Kissinger has told me that American foreign policy is always shifting back and forth between two extremes—either starry-eyed idealism or brooding isolationism. Either we're setting forth on some grand crusade or we're turning our back on the world for as long as we possibly can.

I think Kissinger is absolutely right. Americans have always been missionaries at heart, believing that our good intentions (and good money) will always prevail. We have so much faith in the American Dream that we can't understand why everybody in the world doesn't share our enthusiasm.

Our other tack is to turn away from the big world and hope for the best. The result is that problems sometimes get worse until we're left with no choice but to get involved, usually at a much greater cost than if we'd intervened earlier. The key is prudence—just the right balance of idealism and practical good sense. High ideals and grand plans will get you only so far. You've got to know what's doable and what isn't. You have to know how to bargain.

Ronald Reagan played the major role in ending the cold war. He didn't flinch from calling the Soviet Union an "evil empire," but he didn't flinch from the chance to strike a deal either. He saw his big chance and took it, surprising conservatives and liberals alike.

Many of my friends still wince at the mention of Reagan. They can't face the fact that he proved them wrong about a lot of things. Here was a man dismissed as an amateur and practically a public menace—remember when Reagan was "the cowboy" about to get us into nuclear war?—who was bold enough to announce that the communist world could not only be contained but also defeated. These days they like to ascribe his achievements to luck. But that's nonsense. Nobody's luck is that good. No, Reagan won because he believed in America, and believed in toughing it out, even when under fire from his critics. He had the nerve to craft his policies toward dominance, always with his eye out for the right deal. Reagan recognized in Gorbachev a man willing to shake things up—primarily because Gorbachev was smart enough to see that his country was already well down the tubes. Anybody who believes that the Berlin Wall would have come down if Mondale were elected in 1984 doesn't deserve to be taken seriously.

But despite what the experts say about the post–cold war world, we have not reached the end of history. Quite the contrary. We're the biggest and best and everybody wants a piece of us. The years ahead will be filled with challenges, challenges made all the more difficult by the failure of those in the political game to talk straight. If we are blindsided by crises, we are more likely to make poor choices. If we pay attention, and act like a hardheaded, self-confident superpower instead of a high school guidance counselor, we'll be rested and ready, even when the inevitable crunches come.

HOW TO TAKE ON CHINA

Our biggest long-term challenge will be China. Obviously China isn't the miserable place it was under Chairman Mao. But the massacre at Tiananmen Square was only ten years ago and, despite the world's outrage, the Chinese people still have few political rights to speak of. China is a different place today and we should all be grateful for that. The Chinese people certainly are.

Chinese government leaders, though they concede little, desperately want us to invest in their country. Though we have the upper hand, we're way too eager to please the Chinese. We see them as a potential market and we tend to curry favor with them even at the expense of our own national interests. Our China policy under Presidents Clinton and Bush has been aimed at changing the Chinese regime by incentives both economic and political. The intention has been good, but it's clear to me that the Chinese have been getting far too easy a ride.

For years now American CEOs have been jetting back and forth to Beijing bearing the good news of expanded trade and economic reform. I've been throughout Asia. And even a few years ago, among a number of other powerful economies, China seemed particularly impressive, showing signs of tremendous growth and potential. So it's understandable that businessmen come back from China aglow with dreams. One-billion-plus people would be a huge consumer market. Investment in China is a risky business however. Spending and saving patterns are not anything like they are here and personal income is low. I'm not going to be opening a hotel there any time soon, but maybe someday it could happen.

Despite the opportunity, I think we need to take a much harder look at China. There are major problems that too many at the highest reaches of business want to overlook.

There is, as I mentioned, the human-rights situation. The Clinton administration, which does not make a practice of lashing China, nevertheless reports that China continues,

> . . . to commit widespread and well-documented human-rights abuses in violation of internationally accepted norms, stem-ming from the authorities' intolerance of dissent, fear of unrest, and the abuse of laws protecting basic freedoms. The Constitution and laws provide for fundamental human rights, but they are often ignored in practice. Abuses included torture and mistreatment of prisoners, forced confessions, and arbi-trary and lengthy incommunicado detention. Prison conditions remain harsh. The government continues severe restrictions on freedom of speech, the press, assembly, association, religion,

privacy, and worker rights. . . . All public dissent against the party and government was effectively silenced by intimidation, exile, the imposition of prison terms, administrative detention, or house arrest.

This government must not have gotten the word that capitalism has triumphed over oppressive communism and that people just don't act this way anymore.

So why am I concerned about political rights? I'm a good businessman and I can be amazingly unsentimental when I need to be. I also recognize that when it comes down to it, we can't do much to change a major nation's internal policies. Maybe I should do what regular politicians do—overlook principles, ignore human rights and hope for the best. After all, I do believe that the best thing we can do for backward, oppressive nations is to pull them into the trade matrix.

Where I break rank with many business colleagues, and foreign-policy gurus, is in my unwillingness to shrug off the mistreatment of China's citizens by their own government. My reason is simple: These oppressive policies make it clear that China's current government has contempt for our way of life. It fears freedom because it knows its survival depends on oppression. It does not respect individual rights. It is still, at heart, a collectivist society. As such, it is a destabilizing force in the world, and should be viewed that way. We want to trade with China because of the size of its consumer market. But if the regime continues to repress individual freedoms, how many consumers will there really be? Isn't it inconsistent to compromise our principles by negotiating trade with a country that may not want and cannot afford our goods?

Yes, we want to help China expand its economic potential, not only because we want to expand markets, but also because a more prosperous society is much harder to oppress. But we do not want to do so at the cost of fairness to ourselves. Our trade with China is more than just a little one-sided. China sells to the United States about four times what we're allowed to sell in Chinese markets.

Our China deals should reflect this wariness, especially in satellite and missile technology, because those deals might severely compromise U.S. security interests. Many of the deals we've already struck may come back to haunt us.

But nothing China does seems to shake the faith of the foreign-policy experts. They believe that if we just keep giving China almost everything it wants, Chinese leadership will eventually see the light. "To protect its interest in peace and stability, freedom of the seas, and access to markets in Asia," writes Edwin J. Fuelner in the *Washington Times*, "the U.S. must create an environment that encourages China to integrate into the international system as a responsible member." The writer is a conservative, but basically this is the thinking today guiding American policymakers.

The Clinton administration, like the Bush administration before it, follows a policy of "constructive engagement" with China. When China disappoints expectations and ignores lofty lectures, we issue a few condemnations, hammer out some meaningless resolution at the UN (if we can get it by China's UN delegation), and call upon them to comport themselves like citizens of the community of nations. Then we get back down to business as if nothing had happened.

How's this policy working? It isn't. China has been helping itself to top-secret American technology, spying on the American military, supplying nuclear technology to American enemies like Iran and Iraq, threatening American allies like South Korea and Taiwan, breaking one agreement after another (from arms control to copyright protection), compromising America's political campaign laws, flooding American markets with cheap goods produced by forced labor, and pouring $80 billion a year into a world-class military machine that includes nuclear missiles aimed at America.

Sure we can trust them.

Let's look at this very real, and almost totally undiscussed, military threat. Ask any military thinker what country in the world poses the greatest long-term danger to its neighbors or to America. Ask them what country is arming the fastest and spending the most on its military. Ask them what country is closest to America in its nuclear capability. The answer to all three questions is the People's Republic of China.

I recently read the annual assessment of foreign military threats published by our own Office of Naval Intelligence. (This is information more Americans need to be familiar with.) In this particular assessment, Iraq, North Korea, and Libya are mentioned almost as an afterthought. Advanced tactical aircraft, aircraft carriers, and destroyers, surface-to-air missiles, nuclear submarines—you name it and the Chinese are building it. Why? What neighbor of China poses the least threat to its security? Burma? Malaysia? Singapore? There is no getting around the conclusion that China is building a massive offensive force well beyond any reasonable regional need.

Here's something else to keep in mind: When President Clinton went to Beijing in 1998, the Chinese regime made a big show of announcing that the thirteen odd intercontinental missiles it had aimed at the United States would be retargeted elsewhere. The Clinton administration held this out as some sort of big diplomatic triumph. It raised in my mind a simple enough question: Why were those missiles aimed at us in the first place?

And one more question: Where did they get all the technology to do this? The answer is, they got it from us. As I write this, we have just learned that China had a spy planted at Los Alamos. FBI agents found fifty years' worth of U.S. nuclear secrets squirreled away in the spy's computer. We don't know yet how much of this information he had managed to pass along to China, but it looks grim. Our strategic partner has fleeced us.

It's always this way with China. We give the Chinese regime everything they ask for in trade, technology, market access, and cash reserves—and what we hold back they steal anyway. In exchange, a relatively few American corporations, like Boeing, Hughes, and McDonnell Douglas, get to compete with Airbus Industrie and other European corporations in currying favor for Chinese contracts. But what's in it for the average American? Nothing—especially when our security is threatened.

At a UN meeting on human rights not so many years ago, a spokesman for the Chinese foreign ministry accused the United States of being "a moneybag democracy"—all high and mighty in our moral rhetoric, but quick to lay aside principle when there's profit to be had. I think if we're going to call names we should return the favor and identify China for what it is: a growing military threat abroad and an oppressive regime at home. Let's not pretend we're dealing with anything less.

And let's also operate with the understanding that China doesn't aspire to a strategic partnership. It sees us as a rival in its ambition to dominate Asia. Our allies in the region, like Japan and South Korea—to say nothing of Taiwan—see it that way too. Do they fear China? You better believe they do. And for good reason. Listen to the words of one of China's own military planners in a paper prepared for senior Chinese officials called "Can the Chinese Army Win the Next War?" It's quoted by reporters Richard Bernstein and Ross Munro in their informative book, *The Coming Conflict with China:*

> While the conflict of strategic interests between China and the United States was overshadowed for a time by the "tripartite great power" relationship, it is now surfacing steadily since the breakup of the Soviet Union. China and the United States, focused on their respective economic and political interests in the Asia-Pacific region, will remain in a sustained state of confrontation.

We have to make it absolutely clear that we're willing to trade with China, but not to trade away our principles, and that under no circumstances will we keep our markets open to countries that steal from us. If that means losing some big contracts to the French or Germans or whomever, so be it. American foreign policy needs to open the doors for American trade, and not the other way around. Principles and national self-interest here speak with the same voice. There are some things more important than profits, and one of them is our own national security. Let's make money in China, but let's do it the smart way.

China is a big country, and we're familiar with viewing foreign-policy challenges in terms of large nations. But since the end of the cold war we have been forced to deal with a number of smaller enemies who are out of sync with us and with each other. That these nations are small does not mean they cannot inflict a terrible blow to America. Our foreign policy toward these countries, in fact, often seems designed to elicit such an attack.

Instead of one looming crisis hanging over us, we face a bewildering series of smaller crises, flash points, standoffs, and hot spots. We're not playing the chess game to end all chess games anymore. We're playing tournament chess—one master against many rivals. One day we're all assured that Iraq is under control, the UN inspectors have done their work, everything's fine, not to worry. The next day the bombing begins. One day we're told that a shadowy figure with no fixed address named Osama bin-Laden is public enemy number one, and U.S. jetfighters lay waste to his camp in Afghanistan. He escapes back under some rock, and a few news cycles later it's on to a new enemy and new crisis.

Take Kosovo. How many Americans could even have found Kosovo on a map before we led NATO into attacking it? Not only was there little warning to the American people of the military campaign to come, there was also hardly any preparation by our own military. We launched the attack without even having our army and fleet in place. Even if our president's reasons for going in were perfectly sound it *seemed as though* he was trying to divert attention from his personal difficulties. If our military hadn't been so brilliant we could have been in deep trouble in Kosovo. Excellent air power, miserable diplomacy. There's something haphazard, impulsive, and unpredictable about American foreign policy today. Don't feel bad if you're having trouble following world events. Your government can't keep up with them either.

Dealing with many different countries at once may require many different strategies. But there isn't any excuse for the haphazard nature of our foreign policy. We don't have to reinvent the wheel for every new conflict. Yes, the world is much different than it was even a decade ago. Yes, we do face multiple threats we didn't face before. But this isn't to say we are walking in the dark. Instead, we know who and what the threats are. The problem is that we're totally mishandling them.

NORTH KOREA AND OTHER ROGUES

China is our biggest long-term challenge, but in the short term the biggest menace is North Korea. North Korea exports exactly one thing to the rest of the world—trouble. Just about anywhere America is threatened—by terrorists, by the spread of nuclear weapons and missile technology, you name it—we can count on the folks in Pyongyang to have a hand in it. This is no secret. So you have to wonder why our policy toward North Korea is so weak-minded. This is an example of our inability to come up with reasonable policies even when we know exactly where the potential threat is.

We know that our adversaries in North Korea are making weapons of mass destruction. We also know that they will use them if possible because they detest everything about us. So what do we do?

We blink. In fact, we blink so much it looks as though we're asleep. President Clinton has rightly taken some heat on this, but let's be honest: Most of our political leadership shares the blame because, as usual, most of our politicians and pundits are too busy looking at the rainbow to notice the dark clouds moving in.

After we discovered that North Korea was working overtime to build an arsenal of nuclear weapons, Washington demanded the

North Koreans allow an inspection of a reprocessing facility by officials of the International Atomic Energy Agency. Remember, this is the remaining superpower telling North Korea, which is weak, starving, and isolated, to let an international body inspect a suspicious facility.

North Korea's response: No way. They finally agreed to what was called the Agreed Framework, which they signed October 21, 1994, and it was immediately hailed by the Clinton administration as diplomacy at its best. You be the judge. We promised them two nuclear reactors at $4 billion each, up to 500,000 metric tons of fuel oil a year until the reactors come on line, and food for North Korea's masses. In return, North Korea, which is probably the last truly Stalinist regime on earth, promised to halt construction of two Soviet-type reactors, suspend refueling its existing reactor, and allow inspection of spent fuel rods, which can be used to make nuclear weapons.

North Korea knew that we were bluffing. To no one's surprise, a U.S. satellite later found that a large underground complex was being built near the existing nuclear center. This was a huge operation, bigger than similar facilities in Libya, Iraq, and the former Soviet Union. Just to rub our noses in it, they launched a long-range missile a month later. This would not have happened if we'd been tough from the start. Nor did other adversaries fail to draw this conclusion: Uncle Sam is a sap. It was one more example of how far out of the way we will go to avoid confrontation on potential threats. Our enemies learn we don't mean what we say. After we warned China that we would come down hard if they attacked Taiwan, Lieutenant General Xiong Guangkai, deputy chief of China's general staff, responded,

"No, you won't. We've watched you in Somalia, Haiti, Bosnia, and you don't have the will." Iraq saw what happened in North Korea and stiffed our weapons inspectors.

Here is the fundamental difference between Donald Trump and our current crop of presidential wannabes: I do have the will.

Does anyone seriously doubt that North Korea is up to no good? Here you have a pitiful nation, whose people are starving to death, which has nonetheless undertaken an immense nuclear program. When a country this size builds an underground facility bigger than those found in the old Soviet Union, they're serious. So serious is North Korea's leadership that it will clearly risk rebellion by starving masses in order to build weapons of mass destruction. As even the most treacherous dictator knows, a starving population can easily become every bit as dangerous as an invading army.

But still they build.

Which can only mean one thing: This isn't nuclear deterrence on their part. These people want to *use* these weapons if at all possible. Some experts believe they may be close to developing launch systems that could deposit a warhead on our shores, which would certainly threaten U.S. bases and allies.

And we're building nuclear light-water reactors for them.

In reality, North Korea today has the means to do us tremendous damage. Our current "deal" with Korea—a case study in stupidity— has had the usual effect. In August 1998, for example, the people of Japan noticed a strange light passing overhead. North Korea claimed it had sent "a music satellite" aloft in celebration of the communist regime's fiftieth anniversary and formal installation of Kim Jong Il, the creepy son of the late tyrant Kim Il Sung. It turned out to be a multistage nuclear ballistic rocket, a test demonstrating that North Korea now has the technology to devastate mainland Japan.

That's bad enough. Now listen to this. Former defense secretary Don Rumsfeld—a tough, no-nonsense businessman and exceptionally able public servant—was appointed head of a commission to assess the missile threat abroad. One conclusion of the study: "North Korea's ongoing nuclear program activity raises the possibility that it could also produce additional nuclear weapons. North Korea also possesses biological weapons production and dispensing technology, including the capability to deploy chemical or biological warheads on missiles."

Here we have a commission of military and intelligence experts—appointed by the president and Congress to assess the danger of attack from abroad—telling us that, despite all our diplomatic efforts and solemn arms-control agreements, our worst enemy today has the means to attack America and our allies. Worse, we wouldn't even have warning. "It is unlikely," concluded the Rumsfeld Commission, "the U.S. would know of such a decision [to attack us] before the missile was launched. The missile could reach major cities and military bases in Alaska and the smaller, westernmost islands in the Hawaiian chain."

American reaction and diplomacy has been just the opposite of common sense. We essentially seek to buy off the North Koreans by lifting certain economic sanctions in exchange for a temporary freeze on testing of their nuclear missiles. The *Economist* called our policy "acquiescence in serial bribery." Former secretary of state James A. Baker III, a cagey guy I admire, called the agreement "appeasement" and he was absolutely right.

Our North Korean policy is not only bad in itself, it's also a green light to every desperate, angry, brainwashed dictator in every miserable, poor, collectivist state in the world. It completely ignores every major policy lesson of the last century. When we are resolute (as Roosevelt and Reagan were) we win. When we are ambiguous and soft we absolutely invite attack.

What would I do in North Korea? Fair question. It's easy to point out the problem, but what should we do to solve it? Am I ready to bomb this reactor?

You're damned right.

When the Israelis bombed the Iraqi nuclear reactor they were condemned by the world community. But they did what they had to do to survive. The Korean nuclear capability is a direct threat to the United States. As an experienced negotiator, I can tell you that negotiation with these madmen will be fruitless once they have the ability to lob a nuclear missile into Chicago, Los Angeles, or New York. I don't advocate a thermonuclear war, but if negotiations fail, I advocate a surgical strike against these outlaws before they pose a real threat.

Let me be precise and clear. I remember what happened to Barry Goldwater when he advocated the use of nuclear weapons to defoliate the jungles of Vietnam. And I want there to be no media distortion or misunderstanding about my views.

I'm not trigger-happy, nor would I consider the use of force lightly, but as president I would be prepared to order a strike—using conventional weapons—against North Korean targets if it prevented nuclear blackmail or the nuclear destruction of the U.S. population. I'm not talking about an extended air campaign against North Korea, and certainly not a ground war. I'm talking about taking out a very specific target and then returning to the bargaining table. I am advocating such an action only after talks break down—which is highly likely in view of the North Koreans' track record of violating everything they have agreed to thus far.

Doesn't it make at least as much sense to take out these truly threatening facilities as it does to blow up buildings and bridges in downtown Belgrade, Yugoslavia? It would be much smarter to remove a potential threat to this country than to get involved in a civil war in the Balkans, which posed no threat whatsoever to our national security.

We can learn something here from George Bush and see how good a president he was. He wasn't afraid to use American power when he figured out that Saddam Hussein posed a direct threat to American interests in the East. I only wish, however, that he had spent three more days and properly finished the job. It is this kind of will and determination to use our strength strategically that America needs again in dealing with the North Koreans.

A surgical strike would not only put out the fire in North Korea, but it would also send a message around the world that the United States is going to eliminate any serious threat to its security, and do so without apology. Who's going to complain besides China, which is far too interested in trade expansion to do anything more than the perfunctory grousing? Are we afraid we might upset Fidel Castro? Or Iraq? The only thing that unites the people who would oppose such an operation is that they are all nondemocratic regimes who hate the United States because it represents the antithesis of their rotten, corrupt, impoverished police states. Are we going to walk their line, or our own?

When I advocated the possibility of a surgical strike against the North Koreans on *Meet the Press,* moderator Tim Russert asked me about the possibility that nuclear fallout might pollute Asia as a consequence of our taking action. Russert quoted a former secretary of defense saying that a surgical strike was not an option for this reason. After all, Israel attacked a similar facility in Iraq with no fallout. (Within days of the *Meet the Press* broadcast I had two phone calls from officers very high up in our military who both assured me—off the record—that such a strike could be successful. Because both men are still on active duty, neither one wants to be identified.)

The fact is, if we practiced a principled and tough policy toward this and other outlaw states, we wouldn't be in this situation. Even when we finally decide to go after a rogue state, we often stop well short of finishing the job.

Consider Iraq. After each pounding from U.S. warplanes, Iraq has dusted itself off and gone right back to work developing a nuclear arsenal. Six years of tough talk and U.S. fireworks in Baghdad have done little to slow Iraq's crash program to become a nuclear power. They've got missiles capable of flying nine hundred kilometers—more than enough to reach Tel Aviv. They've got enriched uranium. All they need is the material for nuclear fission to complete the job, and, according to the Rumsfeld report, we don't even know for sure if they've laid their hands on that yet. That's what our last aerial assault on Iraq in 1999 was about. Saddam Hussein wouldn't let UN weapons inspectors examine certain sites where that material might be stored. The result when our bombing was over? We still don't know what Iraq is up to or whether it has the material to build nuclear weapons.

I'm no warmonger. But the fact is, if we decide a strike against Iraq is necessary, it is madness not to carry the mission to its conclusion. When we don't, we have the worst of all worlds: Iraq remains a threat, and now has more incentive than ever to attack us.

Am I being contradictory here, by presenting myself as a dealmaker and then recommending preemptive strikes? I don't think so. There's nothing really comparable to unleashing a squadron of bombers, but in the world of business sometimes you have to make quick, secret, decisive moves in order to gain a negotiating advantage. I've done so a number of times, in getting around the objections of would-be landmarks preservation people, in gaining the advantage in trying to secure air rights or a piece of property. Von Clausewitz also said that war is "a continuation of political relations, a carrying out of the same by other means." That makes a lot of sense to me.

Iran is even further ahead of the game than is Iraq. Within five years Iran is expected to have nuclear missiles capable of reaching the continental United States. Like North Korea, China, and Iraq, they've been importing crucial parts and technical assistance from Russia—today the world's nuclear Wal-Mart. Even as the U.S. has tried to save Russia from collapse with loans and IMF bailouts and political support, Russia has become the world's leading exporter of weapons of mass destruction to America's enemies.

BEING THERE FOR ISRAEL

The United States must continue to nurture and safeguard our special relationship with the state of Israel. This relationship must remain the cornerstone of our policy tactics through the entire

Middle East region, as it has been for presidential administrations of both parties for more than half a century.

Why do we have this special relationship? It is not out of charity, guilt, or what some who would attack these bonds have called the political pressure of "ethnic lobbies." We have been there for Israel, as for England, because Israel is there for us. Israel is a stable democratic ally in a region filled with instability and dictatorship. It is an "unsinkable aircraft carrier" for America's interests and values, from the United Nations to the Mediterranean.

Now, as Israel has matured, our close ties also bring America a fair trading partner and a fellow pioneer on the high-tech frontier of medicine and communications that will enrich Americans' lives in the coming century. Our two countries must continue to stand strong together as pillars of freedom and progress.

REHABILITATING RUSSIA

In a way, one has to feel sorry for Russia. It is like an old business or professional adversary who falls on hard times, loses his house, his wife, his money, starts drinking, and is found one day in the gutter. Natural human sympathy makes you want to get the guy on his feet, clean him up, give him a few bucks, and hope for the best.

Our dealings with Russia are, of course, much more complicated. In some ways they are more complicated than they ever were. There are serious debates among foreign-policy experts about who is even running Russia, how much power the Russian military exerts, and whether Russia's elected government can control the sale and export of its nuclear technology. These became urgent questions in late 1998 when the ruble hit the floor and it was unclear that the government would survive. They'll become very urgent questions again soon—count on it.

What I don't understand is why American policymakers are always so timid in dealing with Russia on issues that directly involve our survival. Kosovo was a perfect case in point: Russia was holding out its hand for billions of dollars in IMF loans (to go along with the billions in aid the U.S. has given) the same week that it was issuing threats and warnings regarding our conduct in the Balkans. Imagine if you were at a bank and, while your loan officer was reviewing your application for funds, you took the opportunity to berate him on some unrelated matter. That's basically what Russia was doing. A lot of countries do the same thing. They rely on our generosity on the one hand, while undermining us on the other. We need to tell Russia and other recipients that if they want our dime they had better do our dance, at least in matters regarding our national security. These people need us much more than we need them. We have leverage, and we are crazy not to use it to better advantage.

Few respect weakness. Ultimately we have to deal with hostile nations in the only language they know: unshrinking conviction and the military power to back it up if need be. There and in that order are America's two greatest assets in foreign affairs.

Either we believe in ourselves or we don't. Whenever we involve ourselves abroad, we had better do so with confidence—no more of this Clintonesque apologizing for America and its exercise of authority. Reagan had confidence and the world respected him for it. They knew he meant business. Today, it seems, we do everything half-heartedly, unsure of ourselves even in the use of military power as in Iraq and the Balkans. Better to do nothing at all. As Theodore

Roosevelt put it at the beginning of this century, "A milk and water righteousness unbacked by force is . . . as wicked as and even more mischievous than force divorced from righteousness."

CUBA

Fidel Castro was a thorn in our side even before the time, nearly forty years ago, that he advocated an attack on us by the Soviet Union during the Cuban missile crisis. He's run a nasty and vicious little dictatorship, caused immense suffering to his people, and he talks way too much.

American policy toward Cuba makes no sense. For thirty years Castro has oppressed his people and exported terrorism to Central and South America, as well as bolstered Soviet troops in Angola. What Castro has done to Cuban society is disgraceful: Terror reigns, the secret police are unrestrained, beatings and citizen disappearances are common, and all free expression outside the Communist Party is crushed.

Our program has been to isolate Castro and put extreme economic pressure on him, which, candidly, did not work very well because Castro was receiving enormous financial subsidies from his Soviet patrons. With the fall of the Soviet Union, however, economic hard times have hit Castro's Cuba with a vengeance. The socialist utopia that Castro built has insufficient food, water, electricity, gasoline, rubber, and even lacks everyday commodities such as soap.

More important, the military class that kept Castro in power and previously had access to luxury housing, gasoline, and other amenities is now feeling the economic pinch. Clearly Castro is squeezed as never before and is desperate for hard American dollars to bolster his foundering socialist experiment.

Some would say that we have Castro on the edge of the cliff and now is the time to push him over. After these many years the economic squeeze has worked. That's why I like Senator Bob Torricelli of New Jersey. Although a liberal Democrat, Torricelli is realistic about the dangers of a communist dictator ninety miles from our shores and has been an outspoken leader in the efforts to tighten the screws on Castro through economic embargo.

Incredibly, however, the reaction of the Clinton State Department is exactly the opposite. Now, they tell us, is the time to normalize relations with Cuba and eventually bail Fidel out financially. Nothing could be more wrong.

We like to believe that investment abroad can raise the living standards of third-world people. In Cuba, foreign investors are not allowed to hire or pay Cuban workers. They must pay the government directly for the workers. Castro then pays the workers token salaries in worthless Cuban money and keeps the rest. Under these circumstances, my investment could not help average Cubans—it could only replace the Soviet subsidy Castro no longer receives.

If, for example, I opened a casino/hotel in Havana, I would be required to pay Castro about $10,000 per year for each Cuban worker. But the workers would not benefit. Castro would pay them the equivalent of $10 a month. The rest he'd use to pay for the brutal and violent system that keeps him in power and deprives the Cuban people of basic human rights. In other words, my investment in Cuba would directly subsidize the oppression of the Cuban people. I might make millions of dollars but I'd rather lose those millions than lose my self-respect.

We have to be careful not to fall into the kind of dilemma created by Castro in other parts of the world.

I have noted with interest the efforts of the Spanish to extradite former right-wing Chilean dictator Augusto Pinochet to stand trial for murder and terrorism. Pinochet is no angel but his crimes pale in comparison to the reign of terror unleashed by Castro. In my book, what's good for right-wing dictators is good for left-wing dictators, but you don't hear the human-rights types screaming for Castro's extradition.

That's exactly what I propose. The first time Castro leaves Cuba for any nation that we have extradition treaties with, he should be detained, arrested, and extradited to the United States for indictment and trial on charges of murder and terrorism.

This seems like a much more intelligent course than sending an exploding cigar, as the CIA did in the 1950s. Fidel is a criminal. Let's treat him like one.

I was asked to write my views on Castro for the *Miami Herald* in June of 1999. I said, in part, that I understood the arguments for lifting the Cuban embargo. The cold war is over, Castro is on the ropes. Pumping money into his economy would benefit the long-suffering masses. This is the way, some people argue, to "open up" Cuba: export democracy; this is how to promote entrepreneurship and independence from the state. Each of those arguments is bogus.

Cuba will be freed by ideas, not by rapacious businessmen lining Castro's pockets and propping up his oppressive regime.

Though the cold war is indeed over, it would be instructive to remember the role that Castro played in the struggle between—yes—good and evil. He turned his island over to his Soviet patrons. He was quite willing to have nuclear missiles launched from Cuban soil that would have destroyed American cities. He exported revolution to Central and South America and even to Africa. He abetted Libyan terrorism. He gave asylum to murderers.

Even worse, he turned his nation into a maximum-security prison. His regime controls every aspect of human life: access to food, medical assistance, schools, and employment. Castro has not mellowed with age. Terror continues to reign. The secret police are unrestrained. The disappearance and beatings of citizens are still tools for civilian control, as is the suppression of free speech. Castro's ruthless domination of the Cuban people has not lessened even as his regime crumbles.

When I wrote in the *Miami Herald* about my views regarding Cuba and Fidel Castro I was overwhelmed by the response of the Cuban American community. In South Florida I literally received thousands of cards, letters, faxes, and e-mails from both Cuban leaders and average Cuban American citizens.

Among these letters was one I was particularly pleased about. It was from Jorge Mas Santos, the chairman of the Cuban American National Foundation and the son of Jorge Mas Canosa, the Cuban American patriot who spearheaded opposition to Castro in the U.S. by making sure Americans clearly understood the true nature of the Cuban gulag.

Jorge Mas Santos, who succeeded his father as chairman of the Cuban American National Foundation, is carrying on this tradition of effectiveness on behalf of those who want to return Cuba to freedom and democracy. Jorge Mas invited me to Miami for a reception in my honor sponsored by the Cuban American National Foundation. I was pleased to accept and envisioned a ceremony with ten or fifteen committee leaders. Instead thousands of people turned out. Not just affluent Cuban American professionals, but average citizens too—janitors, seamstresses, housekeepers, and working people who yearn for the return of liberty in their homeland.

Later I was asked by the *Wall Street Journal* to write an op/ed article outlining my priorities as president. In speaking about Cuba I said that I would immediately reverse the move to normalize relations with Castro, calling him the most abnormal political figure in our hemisphere. As I said, we have pushed him to the precipice with our embargo, helped again by the withdrawal of Soviet backing. Now comes a movement, backed by State Department bureaucrats, to rescue Mr. Castro with U.S. dollars. Normalization is pure lunacy. Again I said that if a right-wing leader like Augusto Pinochet can be extradited and tried for his crimes against humanity, the same treatment should be accorded Mr. Castro.

Two days later, former Connecticut governor Lowell Weicker told the American Reform Party conference in Washington that one of his highest priorities, if he were elected president on the Reform Party ticket, would be immediate normalization of relations with Castro's Cuba. What soft-headed liberals like Weicker fail to understand, as I said in the *Miami Herald,* is that economic infusion of capital into Cuba flows only to the government, not to the people.

Weicker said that Radio Martí funding should be cut and the program cancelled. He's dead wrong. It is vital that the people of Cuba know what things are really like in the United States, get some glimmer of how life in a democracy works, and recognize that the anti-American rhetoric that has kept Castro in power for forty years is merely propaganda.

I say we export ideas by expanding communication with the Cuban people. The technical advances of this century make it impossible for Castro to shut out the outside world.

In the end, it is the truth that will set the Cuban people free.

BLOCKHEAD'S GUIDE TO FOREIGN POLICY

Humanitarian concerns, which are sometimes represented as working in our "national interest," are not good enough reasons in themselves for deployment of forces.

Fact one: We don't have a dog in most of the world's dogfights. That's not to say our hearts don't go out to people whose countries are being ravaged by war. Far from it. Our hearts do go out to them, and so does a lot of U.S. humanitarian aid.

But we have no business, and certainly no right, to intervene in conflicts just because we don't like to see innocent people being killed or dislocated. Just after we started bombing the European capital of Belgrade, a poll came out saying that a majority of Americans thought it was our "right" to get into this longstanding and bloody dispute. I disagree.

I, like everyone else, am horrified when I see people mistreating, oppressing, or murdering others. I have been extremely depressed at what has happened in Africa. My heart is with those people because so many of them are so powerless and are swept up in wars that are horrendously bloody by comparison to the wars we see in contemporary Europe (where we seem especially prone to sticking our noses). If you believe in the human family, you cannot look at contemporary Africa without feeling a great deal of anguish.

Yet it should be clear by now that when we intervene in these conflicts we do little more than temporarily tilt the balance of power. Sometimes, as in the Balkan mess, we're allies with one side for a while, then shift our support to the other side. In the first place, we don't have any idea of how to build democracies in these countries, even if such a thing were possible or desired by them. To top it off, we are deploying troops at the same time we are cutting defense expenditures. None of this makes one bit of sense.

All we really know how to do is make a show of our outrage, and even then we are likely to botch the operation. The point was made perfectly in Somalia, where we made a big splash coming in but quickly realized we were in a quagmire of intranational hostilities that we could do nothing to settle. The tragedy was compounded by the loss of American lives, after which we quickly lost interest in the Somali cause and beat an undignified retreat. This debacle hurt our international standing.

My rules of engagement are pretty simple. If we are going to intervene in a conflict it had better pose a direct threat to our interest—one definition of "direct" being a threat so obvious that most Americans will know where the hot spot is on the globe and will quickly understand why we are getting involved. The threat should be *so* direct that our leaders, including our president, should be able to make the case clearly and concisely, which has certainly not been the case regarding the terrible events in Yugoslavia.

Make no mistake, I love the American desire to help others. The American public will give the disadvantaged money and aid with no expectation of return. They give simply because they know it is the right thing to do. We are the greatest of all humanitarian nations.

At the same time, we must not get involved in a long-festering conflict for humanitarian reasons. If that's our standard, we should have troops stationed all over Africa, and much of Asia as well. We will provide humanitarian assistance, but when our men and women volunteer in our armed forces it should be with the strict understanding that they will be sent into danger's way only in cases where our national survival is directly affected. Young people now enlist, thinking they're signing up to protect America, and end up responding to a palace coup in a country few ever heard of.

I am not an isolationist, but neither am I one of those giddy globalists who thinks that we should leave everything to the IMF and the UN. We're not the world's savior—that job is taken—but there are some things we can do and we shouldn't shy from doing them. However, it is essential that we sort out those areas where we have a national interest from those where we do not.

In the Middle East, America must stand by our only ally in the region: the state of Israel. Not only is Israel strategically important in terms of the world's oil supply, but it is also the only democracy in the Middle East. Check Israel's voting record at the United Nations.

The Soviet Union is no longer a threat to our Western European allies. America has no vital interest in choosing between warring factions whose animosities go back centuries in Eastern Europe. Their conflicts are not worth American lives.

Pulling back from Europe would save this country millions of dollars annually. The cost of stationing NATO troops in Europe is enormous, and these are clearly funds that can be put to better use. Our allies don't seem to appreciate our presence anyway. We pay for the defense of France yet they vote against us at the United Nations and choose the side of the North Koreans, the Libyans, and other rogue nations.

But, ultimately, I don't think that we should abandon Europe completely. Pat Buchanan has made headlines for a book in which he says that the allies did not need to go to war against the Third Reich because Hitler's ambitions were modest; he would have been happy simply to conquer Eastern Europe, so the German people would have elbowroom, and would have left the rest of the world alone. Buchanan's position seems to come from that weird cloudcuckooland where left and right meet each other. His recommendation of appeasement toward the Nazi regime sounds exactly like what liberals said about Hitler in the '30s and what liberals today are saying about rogue states like North Korea. If you applied the same doctrine of appeasement to domestic criminals, you'd be giving murderers and armed robbers stern reprimands and setting them free.

IMMIGRATION—PROTECTING OUR OWN

There's another area of foreign affairs that doesn't get talked about very much, but it is a huge issue: Immigration.

America is experiencing serious social and economic difficulty with illegal immigrants who are flooding across our borders. Five million illegals live in this country. Two million of them live in California. Seven hundred thousand undocumented immigrants live in Texas. We simply can't absorb them. It is a scandal when America cannot control its own borders.

Immigrant advocacy groups have no business rising up in protest, demanding special rights, services, and privileges. We can't allow ourselves to welcome outsiders to our shores out of kindness. If people enter this country by disregarding our laws, can we be confident that they will suddenly become law-abiding citizens once they arrive? A liberal policy of immigration may seem to reflect confidence and generosity. But our current laxness toward illegal immigration shows a recklessness and disregard for those who live here legally.

The majority of legal immigrants can often make significant contributions to our society because they have special skills and because they add to our nation's cultural diversity. They come with the best of intentions.

The United States admitted 915,900 new legal immigrants in 1996—195,000 more than the year before. About a fifth of these people came from Mexico and more than half came from Latin America, with most of the balance coming from Asia and Africa. Along with them came a hundred thousand or so refugees—some 40 percent of them from republics of the former Soviet Union and the rest from various other troubled regions of the world. Statistics like these have a lot of people worried—though overall there has been a marked decline in legal immigration since 1990.

Legal immigrants do not and should not enter easily. They have to wait years and go through a lot of aggravation. Go into your local INS office sometime. It's a long, costly, draining, and often frustrating ordeal—by design. People who immigrated here had to really want it. I say to legal immigrants: Welcome and good luck.

But let's be extremely careful not to admit more people than we can absorb.

It comes down to this: We must take care of our own people first. Our policy to people born elsewhere should be clear: Enter by the law, or leave.

As it happens, deportation of illegal immigrants has lately been stepped up. More than a million deportable aliens were apprehended in 1996 and 37,000 criminal aliens were packed off back to where they came from.

But it's still not good enough. It's irresponsible to give a helping hand to outsiders so long as there is one American deprived of a livelihood or basic services.

INTERNATIONAL TRADE

You only have to look at our trade deficit to see that we are being taken to the cleaners by our trading partners. We need tougher negotiations, not protectionist walls around America. We need to ensure that foreign markets in Japan and France and Germany and Saudi Arabia are as open to our products as our country is to theirs.

Our long-term interests require that we cut better deals with our world trading partners. This will raise an outcry, because we've fallen into the habit of mistaking the easy availability of cheap, sweatshop-produced product for solid and sustainable economic stability. America has been ripped off by virtually every country we do business with. We need to renegotiate fair trade agreements. I would put the right people in charge of negotiation and would get involved myself. If President Trump does the negotiating, we'll get a better deal for American workers and their families, and our economy will not be as vulnerable to global pressures as it is today. Watch our trade deficit dwindle.

Our government has a U.S. trade representative. This important job has cabinet rank. You really have to wonder what our trade representative has been doing for the last seven years.

What I would do if elected president would be to appoint myself U.S. trade representative; my lawyers have checked and the president has this authority. I would take personal charge of negotiations with the Japanese, the French, the Germans, and the Saudis. Our trading partners would have to sit across the table from Donald Trump and I guarantee you the rip-off of the United States would end. The American people would benefit in two ways—I'd lower our trade deficits and I'd save the salary of our U.S. trade representative because I wouldn't accept it.

It's become a cliché to say that business, especially trade, is like war. (Many successful books on business have approached the subject that way.) But cliché or not, it's true. Germany and Japan were our enemies in World War II, and for decades afterward each was a powerful competitor in trade—tough in peacetime as each had been in war. (Though both have fallen on lean times recently, they will become worthy adversaries again.) We didn't make the best possible trade deals with them. We're not making smart deals now. I've pointed out the immense mistake we're making in our dealings with North Korea and other rogue states. The core of these problems is that we don't know how to negotiate. We don't know how to get what we want out of the people we're sitting across the table from.

There was a time in the mid-'80s, for example, when the Japanese were overfishing the Pacific. By combining forces and laying down the line, other fishing nations prevailed. The Japanese stopped using their large nets, giving opportunities to fishermen of other nations and, more important, protecting the environment. You have to know how to be just firm enough and how to persist and persist and persist until you get what you want and get it close to the terms you want.

Though we defeated them in war, in peacetime we were never successful in dealing with Japanese governments (which were unstable) or with their banks (which were the biggest in the world). Despite their current difficulties, the Japanese still outdo us in the production of cars, and the Germans are actively buying up U.S. companies.

There are all kinds of opportunities out there. The chaotic nations of the former Soviet Union, a potentially rich but repressive China, an economically united Europe with great potential. But we have to know not only *what* we want but how to *get* what we want—how to make our moves, how to sit still. Politicians hate confrontation because they can't afford to make enemies. They never stop campaigning.

In 1992, in my book *Surviving at the Top*, I proposed a committee of leading public figures—corporate leaders and dealmakers—to sit on a panel that would realign our economic and political relationships with the world. It's still a good idea.

Even a one-term president, who knew how to make a deal, could get this country's trade and foreign affairs in order in a way that would last for a long, long time.

Frankly, there are many aspects of trade where my negotiating skills could be useful.

SPEAK SOFTLY . . .

At the beginning of this century Theodore Roosevelt approached both domestic and foreign battles guided by the West African phrase "Speak softly and carry a big stick." It's still a good MO.

Today we need to begin shaping events instead of waiting for events to shape our policies. Four months before the Serb army moved into Kosovo there was a summary purging of Serbian generals on record as opposing the invasion. What should that have told us? We were negotiating with the Serbs, trying to talk them out of their threats to occupy Kosovo, and when they made good on those threats we weren't even ready. I'm delighted that there was a happy ending in Kosovo, but it could very easily have been otherwise. You can learn a lot from a near miss.

It was the same story in May of 1997 when Americans picked up their newspapers to learn that Pakistan had just tested a nuclear weapon—prompting India to stage a similar test a few days later. Pakistan? Nuclear weapons? We had no clue it was coming. Our own intelligence services learned of the test only when it showed up on seismic monitors. Even the Rumsfeld Commission, in its assessment of the threat from North Korea, Iran, and Iraq, admitted it was relying partly on guesswork. What does that tell you about future threats? Here we are, the lone superpower in the world, and yet we find ourselves taken by surprise in matters concerning our own most vital interests. If we don't address this intelligence gap immediately our foreign policy will always be reactive.

I've learned in the business world that bluster gets you exactly nowhere. Under the Clinton administration our foreign-policy leaders talk too much. Endlessly. Nonstop. Around the clock. As if following some secret strategy to bore our enemies into submission, this administration makes threat after threat after threat. Even when they actually carry out a threat, there they are again in front of the cameras explaining and announcing and issuing still more threats, warnings, and condemnations. When I do a megabillion-dollar business deal I never tell my competitors what I will and will not do.

To tell the enemy we're not going to invade defies common sense. It conveys weakness, lack of discipline, incoherence, and a lack of confidence in our objectives. That lack of confidence may reflect another troubling reality: our diminished military forces. To wage our aerial assault on Yugoslavia we have had to call upon U.S. forces from all points of the globe, from the Persian Gulf to the Pacific. Why? Because we're spread too thin. The United States last year spent about 3 percent of gross domestic product maintaining our military forces—or about $250 billion. Compare that with past figures: Defense spending in the last year of the Carter admin-istration came to 4.9 percent of GDP. During the Reagan buildup it was 6.5 percent of GDP. U.S. defense spending, in other words, is half what it was as a percentage of GDP. We are still living off the Reagan military buildup of nearly twenty years ago. Seventy-five per-cent of our air force planes have been in service for twenty years or longer. The question is: What will we live off ten or fifteen years from now if we do not invest again now?

You can't pursue forward military and foreign-policy objectives on a backward military budget. I'm not advocating that America go forth and police the world. Far from it. I'm just saying that, if we're going to use our military power abroad as we are today, we had better make sure that power is ready to be used.

THE HIGH PRICE OF PEACE

We definitely must find funding for defense, which means somebody is going to come up with less money for their own project. My suggestion is going to rankle some of my more conservative friends, but I think the best place to start is by diverting money from the planned missile defense system. I know this sounds almost counterintuitive, because a missile defense system is supposed to help us defend against attack by rogue states.

To begin with, I'm not laughing at missile defense, and I never have. A lot of people laughed at Ronald Reagan when he announced what detractors pegged as "Star Wars." Reagan is crazy, they insisted, but it's clear now that he was crazy like a fox. The Soviets definitely believed we could build such a system, and the threat of one protecting our cities put them in a much more compromising mood. It convinced them that they were not going to be able to continue competing with us militarily, because we had moved too far out front technologically. Now even the earlier detractors believe such a system is possible, and the president says he sees the time coming when we will need such a system.

The question isn't whether or not such a defense can be built. The question is whether it is the right defense for our times. And I believe the answer is, largely, no. Yes, outlaw regimes like Libya, North Korea, or Syria might eventually develop missile capability, though with better intelligence and the will to act when necessary we can counter those threatening developments. But in this age of miniaturization, our real threat is not going to be flying in on a missile. It's going to be delivered in a van, or a suitcase, or a fire-hydrant-sized canister. I'll discuss that threat in the next chapter.

★　　　★　　　★

We're a nation of industrious, creative, and diligent people, and we deserve what we've made for ourselves. Like everyone else in this country I vastly prefer a soft sofa to a bed of nails.

At the same time, there's no doubt in my mind that Americans would vastly prefer knowing what challenges lie ahead to waking up one morning to the horror of an unforeseen crisis. We can't command the world to go exactly our way, but we can shape events to a degree that is unmatched among other nations.

Our first challenge is to insist that our political leaders and opinion-makers start making these issues central to the national conversation. Yes, I know that many of them will say that Americans aren't interested in foreign affairs. The television people will complain that if a story isn't sexy or violent enough, no one will watch.

Believe me. Once you make it clear how malevolent our adversaries are—and exactly what their weapons can do to our children—you'll have everyone's attention. And it couldn't come a moment too soon.

CHAPTER FIVE

Freedom from Terrorism

YOU THINK THAT TERRORISM ISN'T a problem in this country? All right, say you want to discount the nut-case terrorism that's been going on here at least since the assassination of JFK—lone-gunman terrorism. Or maybe you want a definition of terrorism that doesn't cover the high school killers or Buford Furrow, the White supremacist loser who drove to Los Angeles so he could shoot up a Jewish daycare center. Perhaps you'd like to ignore the mystery figure who blew away eight people in a Texas church, apparently because he needed to express some deep-seated hatred of Baptists. Political terrorism? Not here.

Read the papers. Only a couple of months ago President Clinton gave clemency to eleven members of a Puerto Rican terrorist gang who had served nineteen years in jail. They were responsible for 130 bombings, many of them in bars and restaurants, resulting in six people dead and many more maimed. (At least one of those killed was a police officer. He was the father of two small sons.) But we were told these "freedom fighters" had disavowed violence. Jimmy Carter said so, Desmond Tutu said so. And probably the release would help Hillary's Senate campaign among Puerto Rican voters in New York.

One of the leaders of the terrorist group, Ricardo Jimenez, was interviewed on *Meet the Press*. He was asked by moderator Tim Russert if his group had really been so nonviolent. Given their mode of operation, Russert wanted to know, "Isn't there a pretty strong possibility that innocent people are going to be hurt and killed?"

No, Jimenez said, "you know, I think all precautions were taken, you know, to make sure that all human life was preserved. And in the end the measures were not taken that were necessary by the people who owned those establishments. . . ."

In other words, the deaths and maimings could be blamed on the people who owned or managed the places where the bombs went off.

It's an outrage. Clearly these Puerto Rican killers have neither renounced violence nor expressed any remorse for their actions. It is almost beyond belief that President Clinton, for the sake of his wife's Senate campaign, would release these murderers in order to pander for a few votes in the Puerto Rican community. The Clintons tell us they never discussed the matter and that Hillary's campaign was not a consideration. Do you believe them? I don't.

Hillary's attempt to distance herself from the disastrous decision only compounded the matter. This is Clinton at his ham-handed worst.

Let's take a lesson from this incident. Let's pay attention to the warning given by this "anticolonialist," Jiminez. Let's mind our own stores, restaurants, houses, schools, and churches. Because if we don't there will be more acts of terrorism.

I may be making waves, but that's all right. Making waves is usually what you need to do to rock the boat, and our national-security boat definitely needs rocking.

Let's point fingers. The biggest threat to our security is ourselves, because we've become arrogant. Dangerously arrogant. It's time for a realistic view of the world and our place in it. Do we truly understand the threats we face? And let me give a warning: You won't hear a lot of what follows from candidates in this campaign, because what I've got to say is definitely not happy talk. There are forces to be worried about, people and programs to take action against.

Now.

When we talk about foreign policy we're talking about the *governments* of foreign countries. We face a different problem when we talk about the individual fanatics who want to harm us. As my father always said, when you're on top you've got a lot of people gunning for you. That's basic human nature. The little guy wants to topple the big guy. This attitude has taken more than a few from nowhere to the top. And the world loves an underdog, at least in principle.

Many of the world's populations are made up of underdogs who have big teeth and very nasty attitudes. Millions of people around the globe hate everything about the United States. They don't like Wall Street, Main Street, two cars in your garage, or any other aspect of our national prosperity. They don't like our Constitution, they don't like our Bill of Rights. They don't believe in freedom of speech, freedom of assembly, freedom of religion (except their own), or the freedom to be left alone. They believe that democracy is corrupt, not only in practice but in principle.

Democracy represents diversity. These people think that they've got the one true answer. About everything.

But their greatest displeasure is reserved for our popular culture. They hate everything about it: miniskirts, Mardi Gras, Mickey Mouse, the corner bar, cable television, working women, women who drive cars, Hollywood, Las Vegas, Atlantic City, Sunset Strip, the Dallas Cowboys cheerleaders, the Bud Bowl, ABC, CBS, NBC, CNN, and MTV—and that's just the short list. Some of our adversaries despise all this because they want it and know that they'll never get it. But others truly believe our culture is evil. We can kid ourselves all we want by mocking their references to the Great Satan, but also keep in mind that there is no greater destiny for many people than to deal the Great Satan a major kick in the teeth.

There is one other thing about us they hate. Many of our adversaries do not like our strategic alliances, especially with Israel. There are many, many people who wish both of us would disappear in a nuclear flash or in a cloud of biological poison. And nothing would give them more pleasure than to be the ones to pull the trigger, even if they happened to be sitting on top of the bomb. Remember the movie *Dr. Strangelove*, and the part with Slim Pickens riding the nuke as it falls from the plane? This is real-life fantasy for some of our enemies. Our teenage boys fantasize about Cindy Crawford; young terrorists fantasize about turning an American city (and themselves) into charcoal.

You see my point: Lots of people out there don't like us. But until fairly recently that didn't make much difference, simply because these malcontents didn't have the ability to cause any major damage. Even if a fanatical America-hater happened to be at the controls of a rogue state like Iraq, Iran, or Libya, about all he could do is bomb a disco or a jetliner, take hostages from an embassy, or kidnap tourists. While those were always tragedies (not to mention major media events) they didn't threaten our nation or our way of life. Most of the time, the best the fanatics could do was round up their subjects, harangue them for a couple of hours about how bad America is, then send them back to their dinners of boiled rats and cabbages. When they did strike out in their limited way, they could often count on us returning the favor, as when President Reagan sent bombers against Moammar Ghadhafi. Even Bill Clinton has bombed a few suspected terrorists sites, though the timing was always suspect.

MINIWAR

That was then. Now we face a threat never before encountered, one that can strike without warning and devastate our civilian population. In our age of miniaturization, weapons have shrunk—and the threat against us is suddenly very large. When a nuclear device can fit in a suitcase, and a canister of anthrax can devastate New York, Boston, Los Angeles, or any other American city, the equation has changed radically. While I was writing this book, a guy carried a vial of super-deadly anthrax poison into a congressional hearing room, just to make the same point that my uncle John Trump had made many years earlier.

Uncle John, an MIT professor, didn't think a foreign power was going to send a bomber over the city and drop a conventional weapon. He knew, decades ago, that miniaturization was coming. He talked about a lone fanatic detonating a weapon at Penn Station that would level the whole town.

A biological attack would not take out buildings, but might kill thousands. The city would come to a halt as medical technicians tried to find space for the sick while realizing that most would die anyway. There would have to be new systems devised for the distribution of food, the restoration of businesses, the disposal of the bodies of the dead.

We're in a new ball game, though you'd never know it from the political and media happy chatter. You may not win a standing ovation by pointing out that there are malevolent people lurking in the shadows with biobombs. That would be the responsible thing to do, and it would be nice to think our politicians would be as serious about preparing us for possible disaster as they are about celebrating the stock market's rise. Their chief job, all too often, is to get reelected. They don't want to be the bearers of bad news. For that matter, we rarely hear many ratings-hungry news analysts talking about a subject that is, without a doubt, probably the most frightening of all national scenarios.

Yet it's time to get down to the hard business of preparing for what I believe is the real possibility that somewhere, sometime, a weapon of mass destruction will be carried into a major American city and detonated. To his credit, Ted Koppel in a *Nightline* series devoted to terrorism said, "Most experts within both the civilian and military branches of the federal government are now convinced that it is no longer a question of whether there will be a biological attack against an American city. It is now merely a question of when."

My hope is that if enough of us start talking about this danger, our elected leaders will address it. The longer they avoid this issue, the more vulnerable they make us. We need to enlighten them now.

I've come to two bedrock conclusions about this threat.

First: We need to prepare ourselves not only for the possibility of attack, but also for blackmail. There may be times ahead when Americans are given the choice of either holding on to our way of life—our American Dream—or giving in to a nuclear or biological threat. There may come a time when we are given the choice between keeping our alliances or suffering an attack. For example, Arab extremists may offer this bargain: Cut your ties with Israel or we will strike a major American city. Such a situation will test us to the depths of our souls.

Second: Though it's shocking and difficult to accept, we need to recognize that even if we mobilize we may not be able to stop every attack.

As always, the first line of defense is to try to understand the nature of the threat, then consider how the current leadership is reacting, and finally decide what kind of improvements we need to make. I've got to say from the outset that I have very little confidence in the way our current leadership is playing our hand. I've seen people like our leaders take similar long odds at the casinos. They always leave the tables broke.

We know that there are many nations that would like to go down in history for having sent Manhattan, Washington, Los Angeles, or Miami to its knees. We've seen plenty of suicide bombers blowing up buses in Israel; barracks and embassies around the Middle East, Europe, and Africa; and even buildings here in the United States. We've seen cultists release poison gas in the Tokyo subway. Whatever their motives—fanaticism, revenge—suffice it to say that plenty of people would stand in line for a crack at a suicide mission within America.

In fact the number of potential attackers grows every day. Our various military adventures—some of which are justified, some not—create new legions of people who would like to avenge the deaths of family members or fellow citizens. It is one cost of peacekeeping we should keep in mind.

I am not a hard-core isolationist. While I agree that we stick our noses into too many problems not of our making and that we can't do much about, I strongly disagree with the idea that we can pull up the drawbridge to hide from rogue nations or individual fanatics.

We may overlook the danger created by rogue states because so many of them are small and poor. The combined economy of North Korea, Iran, Iraq, Syria, Libya, and Cuba is around $174 billion, as compared with our $7.6 trillion. The military expenditure for these countries combined is about 5 percent of what we put out for defense.

But people who make this argument are thinking in the past. They're expecting military threats like battleships, standing armies, strategic bombers, and tank columns. They see war as something they can track with a satellite or through binoculars—as if some hostile navy is going to sail into New York harbor and open fire. The poverty and fanaticism of rogue states naturally propels them toward exactly the kind of warfare we're not prepared for.

Here's another thing to keep in mind: Why would a country use a missile against us when it could more easily, cheaply, and safely infiltrate a biobomb squad. In a conventional attack we would have a pretty good idea where a missile is launched from and could retaliate appropriately. Not so with a human delivery system. Our adversaries may be fanatical, but they're not out to destroy their own countries.

Not appreciating the new, real military dangers is like not knowing about the Internet.

We should think of the threat not in terms of shells, bullets, and missiles, but as something that is almost invisible and that can penetrate any conventional defenses and borders without detection, then do its dirty work. We should think of the threat as a virus.

There is no doubt that rogue states like Libya and Iraq have more than enough resources to develop miniaturized weapons of mass destruction, especially in the post–cold war environment, where former Soviet weapons experts are always looking for jobs and don't care who signs the paycheck. But it doesn't take a nation to develop weapons of mass destruction. As defense expert James H. Anderson reminds us in a Heritage Foundation report, the Japanese cult responsible for the 1995 terrorist attack with sarin gas on the Tokyo subway was a very small group, Aum Shinrikyo.

The key element was dedication. The cult not only bought a 48,000-acre spread in Australia to test their weapons on livestock, but also sent members to Africa to get samples of Ebola virus. The cultists also built two research centers. These same people, by the way, were planning on hitting the U.S.

Now, if a small group of cultists can strike one of the more sophisticated cities in the world, why would anyone believe that a government with more resources—Iran, Iraq, North Korea, and such—couldn't do immensely more damage to us? In fact, why believe that a cult similar to Aum Shinrikyo couldn't do the same thing to the New York system? It's not as if we have any shortage of cults inside our country whose behavior cannot be accounted for by any rational means.

You can be assured that right now there are fanatics, whether they sit in the counsels of doomsday cults or in the cabinets of rogue states, who are plotting and waiting for their moment to strike. The question then is What can we do to best protect our cities?

A lot more than you might think.

THE TWENTY-FIRST-CENTURY SPY

All business success is based on acquiring information, so maybe I have a natural interest in intelligence. One of our most important tools is as old as humanity itself. That tool is the spy. We need to train and employ a lot more of them. We need to be shelling out a lot more money for what the experts call "human intelligence"—which is to say, informants who live and operate within the rogue nations, who join cults of zealots, and who know the shadowy underworld in which our enemies often operate.

Do I believe spies can save us from a biobomb?

Not every time. But one of the ironies of the war against ultra-high-tech, miniaturized weapons is that our best defense isn't high-tech satellite surveillance, but good old-fashioned intelligence-gathering done by agents who are trained in the serious work of infiltrating terrorist groups. In cop terms, we're talking about a gumshoe operation—beating the bricks for information. Nothing fancy about it, but ultimately we could minimize danger by the strategic deployment of shoe-leather.

Because the potential losses are so huge, we should be willing to spend whatever is necessary and reasonable on the preventive side. After all, how do you put a price on the life of a great American city?

Unfortunately, we have a lot of psychic capital invested in high-tech surveillance, and as a result have let our intelligence capabilities shrink. Reversing this trend won't be easy. In Washington, in the budget battles, the flashy hardware usually has the upper hand. James H. Anderson puts it this way:

> Our penchant for technological means has crowded out the development of human intelligence capabilities. The revitalization of human intelligence capabilities is long overdue. Satellite surveillance is wonderful, but it is no substitute for eyes and ears on the ground to ascertain enemy intentions.

This same point is made by former Reagan State Department official Abraham Sofaer in *Five Ways to Beat the Thugs:*

> It is widely agreed that the United States lacks sufficient human intelligence capability. Penetrating groups of radicals and religious fanatics is difficult and distasteful. But it is by now familiar work, and great successes have been achieved, such as preventing an attack on the visa line at the U.S. embassy in Paris in 1968 and other attacks planned at around that time. Congress should keep the pressure on the CIA and FBI to strengthen these capabilities.

Pressure couldn't come a second too soon. Sofaer tells a story of incompetence that hits very close to home:

> The inadequate use of intelligence is pervasive. When, in 1990, El Sayyid Nosair was arrested for the murder of Rabbi Meier Kahane, the FBI failed to translate papers found in his

home because its New York office had no Arabic translator available. Those papers contained useful leads that might have enabled the FBI to prevent the 1993 World Trade Center bombing.

That's bad enough. After all, there are a lot of Arabs who just don't like us. It would follow that our antiterrorist squad would keep a few people around who could read Arabic. They didn't plan.

But , Sofaer says, the story gets worse:

When the mastermind of the Trade Center bombing, Ramzi Yousef, entered the United States with a false passport, he was caught by the Immigration and Naturalization Service but released because the government lacked space in a local facility to hold him pending deportation. He then disregarded orders that he appear for a hearing and went about successfully arranging the Trade Center bombing.

We talk a lot in this society about warning signs, whether at public high schools, which have their own internal terrorist problems, or in the nation at large. If we would acknowledge the threat we face, we wouldn't allow suspicious people to enter our country on a false passport. We would find room to jail guilty people. We would do that because we knew we are vulnerable to attack. If we were taking this threat seriously, this particular bombing probably wouldn't have happened.

Identifying a problem is just part of the political game. The real fight is in coming up with the money to pay for the fix. Where do we find the funding necessary to pay for the human intelligence that may prevent a madman from destroying a U.S. city?

There's no doubt in my mind that once the American people are awakened to this threat, they'll be willing to pay for any reasonable means of defense. In fact, I bet if I started a national-defense lottery, with money earmarked for preventing terrorism against U.S. cities, we would take in enough money to hire and train every spy on earth and still have money to spare. Imagine this for a second: The (Trump) National Security Lottery would sell tickets just like in a Powerball Lottery, but dedicate every cent to funding an antiterrorism campaign. Talk about a good reason to buy a lottery ticket.

To give us the best chance possible to avoid an attack, we have to raise peoples' awareness. That's another reason why a lottery wouldn't be a bad idea. Redirecting missile-defense money to human intelligence would also serve a public relations role by reminding the public that this threat is real and that we're going to spend some real money on it—defense money. The linkage would be important.

BIOTERRORISM

According to the Department of Defense, as reported in a policy analysis from the Cato Institute, five pounds of anthrax could wipe out half of Washington, D.C. You can't defend against that with satellites and laser beams. This is the irony of our times: high-tech threats require low-tech defenses.

But there are some means of attack that seem nearly impossible to defend against. Recently in New York there has been a breakout of an extremely rare type of encephalitis never before seen in this country. It is transmitted through diseased crows that are bitten by mosquitoes that then bite humans. The fever appears to come from the West Nile, but no one has a theory as to how it arrived. A massive spraying campaign was undertaken in the city to kill mosquitoes.

This sounds like one of those odd, nasty tricks nature plays. The director of the city's emergency management office, and the Federal Centers for Disease Control and Prevention, called it a purely natural phenomenon. But the CIA reported that an Iraqi defector claimed that Saddam Hussein was developing a strain of the virus for use in a bioterrorism campaign. The defector, Mickhael Ramadan, had an excerpt from his book published in the *London Daily Mail* in April 1999.

We need to be aware of dangers like these and be prepared for them.

I want to pass along a few more ideas about responding to bioterrorism that I've come across in my reading:

- We need to stockpile antibiotics in major population areas and train emergency workers to respond quickly to biological attack. Perhaps some of those people in the criminal justice system who are doing community service could learn emergency response.

- We need to develop and deploy sensors in major cities that will give us early warning that biological devices have been detonated. Remember, these microbes can take a while to spread, so any warning we have will help to save lives— perhaps tens of thousands of them.

- We need to keep a very close eye on former Soviet biotech-
  nicians, offering them jobs where we can and steering them
  clear of terrorist regimes. Call your congressman. When
  private citizens start asking about the Joint Statement on
  Biological Weapons, politicians will know this is an issue
  they'd better start taking seriously.

- Prepare for the possibility of attack, to avoid total panic in
  case an attack does occur. Our adversaries understand that if
  they are able to blindside us they will be much more likely
  to succeed in blackmailing us.

★   ★   ★

This is all very grim material, and if I were playing it safe, trying to
make people feel good—if I were hoping to offend nobody or concerned about fundraising—I'd keep these thoughts to myself. I'm
telling you the hard truth because, unlike almost all other public figures, I can afford to be truthful.

There will be people who will say that Trump is hardly in a position
to lecture the nation on the perils of modern warfare. Where does a
real estate guy get off thinking he is a prophet on national defense?

But who *are* the experts and what have they done for us lately? It
doesn't take a rocket scientist to understand that we are living in very
dangerous times. It does take courage to say so. And it doesn't take a
brain surgeon to find possible solutions. All it takes is a willingness to
become informed and a desire to be part of the solution. Unlike
other candidates, I'm in a position to bring these issues to the fore-
ground and it would be wrong not to do so.

CHAPTER SIX

An Economic Boom
for America

POLITICIANS ARE ALWAYS TINKERING WITH the tax code and haggling about the federal budget. While it is true that we have a healthy surplus right now, no one has put forward a plan to make this country debt-free as we enter the next millennium.

The plan I propose does not involve smoke and mirrors, phony numbers, financial gimmicks, or the economic chicanery you usually find in Disneyland-on-the-Potomac.

Here is the Trump plan. The editorial-page writers and TV opinion-makers will hate it, but I believe it is bold, radical, realistic, and doable.

I would impose a *one-time,* 14.25 percent tax on individuals and trusts with a net worth over $10 million. For individuals, net worth would be calculated minus the value of their principal residence.

That would raise $5.7 trillion in new revenue, which we would use to pay off the entire national debt.

We would save $200 billion in interest payments, which would allow us to cut taxes on middle-class working families by $100 billion a year or $1 trillion over ten years.

We could use the rest of this savings—$100 billion—to bolster the Social Security Trust Fund. By 2030, when the Social Security fund is expected to go broke, we could put $3 trillion into the trust fund. This would make it solvent through the next century.

Dr. Allen Sinai, chief global economist of Primark Decision Economics and one of the most accurate and respected economists in the country today, discussed my plan with Diane Sawyer on *Good Morning America*. He said, "[The] ideas are intriguing. It is a major redistribution if [the plan is] phased in from the wealthy and the high-income rich and superrich to middle-income America, and we remove the inheritance tax, which is a plus, and we cut the national debt." Referring to the new revenues raised, Sinai was cautious about my assumptions but said, "We don't really need all of that, because we're going to have quite a large amount of surpluses anyway with current law, and so we don't need to have that big a tax cut. So I think it's worth looking at in terms of ideas.

"What the impact might be on the economy and in the election of 2000 [is unclear]. But we have to decide as a nation what to do with budget surpluses, how to deal with Social Security in the long-term sense. It's worthy of examination and consideration."

Great. Sinai is a smart guy—the top analyst and forecaster of financial markets for the United States and international economies.

My proposal would also allow us to entirely repeal the 55 percent federal inheritance tax, which hurts farmers, small businessmen, and women most.

Think about the guy in Jersey City with a dry cleaning business. He and his wife work hard their whole lives to build a successful small business. They have three children they want to leave it to, but under the current tax laws Uncle Sam will get most of it.

Or think about the family farmer in Iowa who tills the soil and subjects himself to the unpredictability of the weather and manages to turn a profit and build a nest egg. He'd like to pass it on to the next generation of family farmers, but once again the IRS will get the biggest bite and leave them almost nothing.

The inheritance tax is a particularly lousy tax because it can often be a double tax. If you put money into trust for your children, you pay the inheritance tax upon your death. When the trust matures and your children go to use it, they're taxed again. It's the worst.

The rich will scream. Only the top 1 percent of people—those with a net worth of $10 million or more—would be affected by my plan. The other 99 percent would get deep reductions in their federal income taxes.

The pundits and editorial-board writers will warn of dire consequences resulting from my proposal—a stock market crash, a depression, unemployment, and so on. Notice that the people making such objections would have something personal to lose. Many of the doomsayers work for wealthy special interests.

It is nonsense to say my plan would bring about a stock market crash. When we pay off the national debt, we would retire all government bonds. People would be able to invest in free enterprise instead of investing in government. This would free up enormous capital that would rush into the stock market. People would invest in America's great companies: General Electric, General Motors, IBM, and Conseco.

Capital would also flood into private equities. Our economy would be zooming.

Nor would my plan cause capital to flee the country. The opposite is true. Paying off our debt and cutting taxes would cause such an economic boom that no one smart would walk away from the opportunities. Interest rates would be low, capital would be plentiful, and opportunities would be everywhere.

And let me say a word about those interest rates. Snuff the national debt, and mortgage rates, credit-card interest rates, and the prime rate would plummet.

I believe that with no national debt and with deep cuts in income taxes, America would experience a 35–40 percent boost in economic activity—the greatest economic boom in our history. We would leave the Europeans and Asians in the dust and maintain our superpower status for the next century.

The increase in economic activity, and more income in the pockets of the American people, would mean more business start-ups. More employers means more employees, more employees means more taxpayers, more taxpayers means more revenue, more revenue means more funding for education, healthcare, infrastructure, Medicare, and other vital programs . . . more business in general.

Speaking of Medicare, having watched my parents lose strength as they aged and having witnessed my father's battle with Alzheimer's only firmed my resolve that the richest country on earth must provide the finest healthcare for our elderly. It would be expensive, but if my debt-reduction plan were enacted we would be able to afford it. First I say fix Social Security, and then shore up Medicare and Medicaid.

Equally important, the psychological benefit to the American people of being debt-free would liberate all of us. There would be an explosion of spirit that would boost the economy and renew business, arts, government, and all the other elements of our society. Ronald Reagan was right when he said America's best days are ahead of us.

It's a win-win idea for the American people but an idea no conventional politician would have the guts to put forward. I'm prepared to fight for it and I recognize that my critics will do everything possible to distort and belittle my plan.

That's why I posted a Web site on the Internet where any American can read a full explanation of my plan. (You can see it at www.DonaldJTrump2000.com. I urge you to check it out.) For those who attack my plan I ask you this: Where's the Bush plan? Where's the Gore plan? Where's the McCain plan? Where's the Bradley plan? And parenthetically, where's the Buchanan plan? Pat may be rubbing two sticks together in his cave trying to light a fire by which he can devise troglodyte blueprints for America.

The special interests will fight my plan, but I believe it would prove so popular with the American people that Congress would fail to pass it only at their own peril. As the late Senator Dirksen of Illinois once said, "When they feel the heat they see the light."

Some will say that my plan is unfair to the extremely wealthy. I say it is only reasonable to shift the burden to those most able to pay. We already have a graduated tax system where people who make more and have more pay more. In fact from 1913, when the income tax was enacted, until we needed money for World War II, the system had *only* taxed the rich. Taxes on everybody are a post–World War II outrage.

The wealthy actually would not suffer severe repercussions. The 14.25 percent net-worth tax would be offset by repeal of the 55 percent inheritance-tax liability.

In fact the boom we would set off would allow any smart entrepreneur to make it back in spades. I know I would.

Most of the truly wealthy people I know—and I know many—have doubled their net worth in the last few years. Yes, I believe we have an obligation to pay. Taxes represent the cost of freedom and its defense. It is a small price.

This plan would cost me $700 million personally in the short term, but it would be worth it. Pat Buchanan wrote that I should start with a $700-million donation to the government. I would if Pat would match me dollar for dollar. I've seen his CNN contract and I know he's got the dough. (I always find it amusing that Pitchfork Pat campaigns as an outsider when, in fact, he's been a card-carrying member of the establishment since Nixon brought him to Washington, and he now lives in a mansion in tony McLean, Virginia.)

I don't want to jolt the country the way Bradley did with his crazy Tax Reform Act of 1986, which killed real estate, banking, and caused the S&L crisis. Allowing the rich to pay over a short time would make our plan go smoothly and would light the fuse for the greatest economic blastoff we've ever had.

If I were elected president of the United States I could, with the strong support of the American people, persuade the leaders of Congress to enact this plan. I know politicians and I know how they think. I've had to deal with them all my life and I think I've exhibited the rare ability to get things done. I could get a good deal for the American people.

I know many very talented economists besides Dr. Sinai. The ones that I've consulted with—you'll know their names when I appoint my economic advisory counsel—have said that this plan is "brilliant."

Why should it be surprising when a good tax plan comes from a developer? I spend a lot of time thinking about taxes, and not just because the Trump hotels/casinos have made me one of the biggest taxpayers in New Jersey. To be a successful builder in America today is to get a crash-course Ph.D. in tax policy. Tax incentives and disincentives affect everything I do, including where I build and how I structure my deals, so what I say about taxes is based on personal experience. But taxes are a thorn in all of our sides. To see why my proposal makes sense you have only to look at the stupidity of the present tax system and its influence on our everyday lives.

Let's start with incentives.

All around the country, from Peachtree Street in Atlanta to Mulholland Drive in Los Angeles, the tax code is shaping and reshaping our country.

You can see this if you take a drive across the country. See an ostrich farm? One big write-off. See a mansion on a hill? Made possible by the recent capital-gains-tax cuts. Spot a crack house beside a freeway? Any self-respecting landlord would raze it and build a nice single-family townhouse. But when property taxes are too high, no family in that neighborhood could afford to live in a more expensive home. So the shack remains.

Lowered taxes sparked redevelopment and booming business in blighted areas like Baltimore's Inner Harbor and New York's Times Square. During the Koch-Dinkins years, a toxic blend of high property taxes and rent control kept whole areas of New York City in a state of disgraceful disrepair.

Taxes can have the same influence on our willingness to work harder, to take a risk in a new venture.

INCOME TAXES ARE NOT A NATURAL PHENOMENON

We are not genetically coded for taxes. We have the power to make the system rational. Despite all the talk of "scrapping the code," and the promises we've heard from Bill Clinton and the Republicans in the Congress, we still have a tax code in this country that is disastrous. *Reader's Digest* says that the IRS now collects more than $1.48 trillion—yes, that's with a "t"—a sum larger than the entire economy of Great Britain.

Middle-class wage earners pay rates that used to be paid by millionaires. The tax code has grown so complex that millions of us have to pay specialists to prepare our returns. And even with the best advice money can buy, we still can't rest easy. The code is so convoluted that even the IRS can't understand it. IRS agents who answer the bureau's advice line often give different answers to the same question. We all know that the code is too complex.

How complex is it? According to a report by Representative Dick Armey and Senator Richard Shelby, the tax code today includes 480 tax forms—and then an additional 280 forms to explain the first batch. Shelby, by the way, is one of the smartest and most effective guys in Washington. Boy, does this guy stand out when you look at some of the losers inside the Beltway. Come to think of it, Shelby would be a great secretary of defense.

Every year the IRS disburses eight billion pages of forms and instructions. If you were to take these forms and lay them end to end, you'd have a government-produced paper trail that would circle the earth twenty-eight times, according to some witty speechwriter for George Bush. So incomprehensible is our tax code that every year American taxpayers walk away from billions of dollars they could get back in refunds. That averages out to about $700 for every man, woman, and child in this country.

Americans are stretched to the breaking point on the tax rack. According to the Tax Foundation, a median-income, two-earner family pays nearly $23,000 or roughly 38 percent of its income each year in federal, state, and local taxes. That is more than the typical family pays for food, clothing, housing, and transportation combined.

You shouldn't have to pay more to Uncle Sam than you pay for the basic necessities for yourself and your children. But you do. And that's a scandal.

Of course taxes get a lot worse if you work hard and climb the ladder to make about $60,000 a year. Then the government's cut of your income rises to 36 percent. And every time you go to the store, buy a Happy Meal, fill your car with gas, go fishing, pay your mortgage, or drive to work on a toll road, the tax man gets another chance to dip his hand into your pocket.

Dean Stansel of the Cato Institute broke out the hidden costs of taxes that workers have to pay today—taxes that you probably never knew you were paying. In all, more than one-quarter of every dollar employers pay to keep an average manufacturing wage-worker on their payrolls goes to the government in the form of various taxes, including payroll taxes, unemployment insurance taxes, and workers' compensation.

Regulatory costs amount to another form of taxation. Your employer likely pays a fortune to keep on the right side of thousands of environmental, labor, safety, equal employment, and other federal regulations. This, by the way, is a developer's nightmare.

In 1996, complying with just the federal government's regulations was estimated to have cost roughly $688 billion. That's about $6,800 per family. Another estimate is that the burden of federal regulations is from $3,000 to $4,000 per employee, or about $1.40 to $2.00 per hour for a full-time worker.

HIGH RATES DISCOURAGE PROGRESS (AND PEOPLE)

We don't have our dream handed to us. We build it. We have our vision, then we go out and make it real. Yet the tax system clearly punishes the nation's dreamers, big and small. That's why the Trump debt-reduction tax plan would benefit the American Dream.

Most people are not going to take time away from their families and work themselves to exhaustion trying to make more money if the government takes such a large cut of their profits. High taxes are a levy on human achievement and a subsidy for mediocrity.

The code also punishes savings and encourages freewheeling consumption. I already know what my critics are saying: Trump shouldn't complain about consumption. After all, he builds and manages casinos, which depend on people spending their money on entertainment.

Touché? Not quite. Clearly I think it's great that Americans are at a place where most of us have what was once called "mad money"—some extra cash for entertainment. The Trump casinos have been honored for the programs we have put in place to assist in the fight against gambling addiction. Gambling is legal, regulated, and for many people provides an outlet for entertainment. But I don't advocate that anyone get in over their head or spend this week's grocery money at the blackjack tables. You shouldn't engage in gambling until your basic needs and obligations have been taken care of.

The trouble is that the tax code steers dollars away from savings and investments and into spending, and we need to encourage more savings in this country. Plus, of course, it robs American families of disposable income.

We have a tax system that punishes the middle class for wanting to join the investment class. First we pay taxes when we earn money. Then we pay again when the money is invested and we make a capital gain.

What high rates and multiple taxation do to personal dreams, high property taxes do to our cities. Through the 1970s and 1980s I watched insanely high property taxes create a disincentive for developers and landlords to refurbish and repair decaying properties. As a result, New York City's government began the dismantling of the world's greatest city. A vibrant area like Times Square, which had once been the very heart of the city, decayed into one big outdoor porno bazaar. Grand old buildings that had once housed the rich and famous became burned-out homes for winos and squatters. Landmarks became eyesores.

The problem of high property taxes still plagues many parts of the country. Here's what Governor Jesse Ventura had to say about Minnesota in his first State of the State address:

Property taxes no longer are tied to the services that are delivered. . . . We have created a so-called "progressive" tax based on the value of property. It punishes people for doing the right thing. If I keep up my property, my value and taxes go up even though I don't need as many local services as the property that has been allowed to deteriorate and needs inspections, fire protection, or police patrols. It's time to quit taxing senior citizens out of homes that they own, [forcing] them into nursing homes or assisted living.

He's absolutely right. The Trump plan would guarantee seniors enough to live on through their retirement. As I noted earlier, my plan would actually fund the Social Security Trust Fund through the next century.

The code also punishes marriage. You'd think that, in a country in which a third of all children are born out of wedlock, the government would do all it could to encourage stable families. Under the current tax laws, a married couple with separate incomes pays a higher tax than they would pay if they were allowed to file as single taxpayers. And married people have to cope with taxes that are vastly more complicated than do single filers.

These costs, both in money and in dealing with a ridiculous level of complexity, constitute a "marriage penalty." For about two-thirds of all married couples the smartest thing they could do, from a tax perspective, is to get divorced. It is bad social policy, and it is just plain wrong.

"THE PARAMILITARY PERFORMANCE OF THE IRS"

After a one-time, 14.25 percent, net-worth tax on the very rich, and the restoration of our country to a sound economic footing, we would need to refine details of the tax system to remove the inequities and absurdities in the tax code. The sheer complexity of the code makes it easy for well-intentioned, law-abiding people to appear to be tax cheats. To make matters worse, rulings by the U.S. Supreme Court allow the IRS to seize your property, your cars, your personal computer or boat, your bank accounts, even your house, with no trial or verdict from a judge.

Take the case of Richard Gardner, a tax preparer in Oklahoma. According to Albert Crenshaw in a *Washington Post* story, Gardner told a Senate investigating committee that he was called out of a meeting one morning in 1995 only to find himself facing fifteen IRS agents and a half-dozen U.S. marshals wearing jackets with bright letters and armed as if they were ready to take down Manuel Noriega.

They seized the records of his clients, as well as his computers, and held onto them for two years. He later found out that the IRS demanded that his clients wear hidden microphones. "It appears the IRS wanted a high-profile 'guilty even if you're not' victim to scare other tax preparers and taxpayers," Gardner said. You can imagine the state of his business after the IRS had worked him over.

W. A. "Tex" Moncrief Jr. owned a family-run oil company in Fort Worth. He told the committee that agents "stormed the offices like an army landing on an enemy beachfront. . . . My employees heard the agents shout, 'IRS! This business is under criminal investigation! Remove your hands from the keyboards and back away from the computers. And remember, we're armed!'"

Worse for Moncrief, the feds had tipped off the local media, so he had his reputation and that of his business dragged through the mud in front of the whole community. Moncrief had to spend $5.5 million on his defense.

Remember that this happened in America.

Years ago the arbitrary treatment of taxpayers by the IRS was a fringe issue. Now it is a matter of concern for some of the brightest and most responsible voices on Capitol Hill. "We have much to be concerned about the paramilitary performance of the IRS," New York's Daniel Patrick Moynihan said at a Senate Finance Committee Hearing in 1998. "It's government violence directed against citizens."

The IRS, in the name of catching tax cheats and liars, has itself cheated and lied.

A New York priest, Monsignor Lawrence F. Ballweg, was a trustee for a charitable trust set up by his mother's will. Somehow, the IRS held him responsible for an $18,000 bill. He received a stream of unrelenting threats from the IRS that made this man of God tremble and shake.

"For eight months I lived in constant worry, if not fear, that the trust that my dear mother had established to help the poor would be penalized because of what I can only call the unprofessional, callous, and indifferent behavior of IRS employees who are devious enough to never sign their names to any notices they fill out," the monsignor told a congressional committee.

"On the surface, the IRS Reform Bill is simply about reforming a government agency," said Arizona Senator John McCain. "But this bill is about more, it is about fundamental fairness and the role of the government in our lives."

The Senate was told that the IRS pursues unofficial tax quotas, putting intense pressure on agents to wring out money from taxpayers wherever they can find it. And whom do they single out? It's not the rich. The rich can hire tax lawyers and defend themselves. No, they often target the middle class and working poor, people who don't have the resources for an extended fight and who'll pay up just to get off the hook.

BOTTOM LINE

Like other large government programs, the tax system has attracted the attention of a number of reformers, many of whom have good ideas. After the national debt is paid off we will want to examine a few of the innovations being discussed about taxes. But first let me sum up everything that's wrong with the tax code. What we all need to do, whether when talking to senators and congressmen or attending town hall meetings or other political events, is to keep these issues in play:

- The tax system is too complex, bleeding off hundreds of billions of dollars and billions of productive hours from the American people.

- Tax rates are still too high, taking too big a bite from the extra dollars people can make.

- Hidden taxes take even more; a government pickpocket you never notice.

- High property taxes punish people for improving their property.

- Our code discriminates against married people.

- Despite the recent reining-in of the IRS by Congress, the sheer volume and complexity of the code allows too much government intrusion into our lives.

- Moreover, the code is liable to change overnight in ways that could jeopardize your plans for a small business or retirement.

Little wonder that one of the most powerful social movements of our time is tax reform.

A NOTE OF CAUTION

Before we make a move on more extensive tax reform, let me warn that we should never forget the experience of the Tax Reform Act of 1986, which showed how an abrupt change could throw the whole economy into a tailspin. This brings me to one of my least-favorite subjects: Bill Bradley.

Bradley is seen by many as the Democratic Party's white knight. They actually prefer him to Al Gore. I have studied both closely. I know their thinking and I know their records of public service. My conclusion: Anyone who prefers Bradley to Gore is either completely ignorant or a member of the family. Let me explain why.

Bill Bradley, presidential candidate of big ideas, is not the outsider he purports to be. For one thing, he's a former U.S. senator from New Jersey. He was also a member of the Senate Finance Committee whose biggest idea was an unmitigated disaster. That big idea was tax reform. The good part of this legislation—it cut taxes in half—can be attributed to Ronald Reagan. The rest must be attributed to Bradley, who voted for major tax hikes not once but twice in the decade that followed the enactment of the Tax Reform Act. Bradley destroyed the real estate industry and caused a deep and lasting depression, and almost single-handedly sank the savings and loan sector. He screwed up more banks than all the Jesse Jameses and Machine Gun Kellys who ever lived.

Businesses make billion-dollar decisions based on the tax code. When you make a sweeping change in that code overnight, it puts the entrepreneur in a bad spot.

Bradley's mistake slammed the real estate markets. Small realtors got crushed. People who were banking their retirement on a condo or a house saw their dreams destroyed. It was also a hard time for developers like me. I hunkered down, survived, and eventually thrived. Many of my competitors, and the contractors, builders, and workers who depended on them, went under. Meanwhile, savings and loan companies, which had been encouraged by the tax codes to invest in real estate, suddenly found themselves saddled with unproductive assets. The result? Taxpayers were hit with a $130-billion tab.

This was Bill Bradley's big idea?

Worst of all, Bradley's big idea cost hard-working people. Many who saved and invested in IRAs, while also contributing to a retirement plan at work, found their IRAs curtailed. "The tax bill was an error," a financial planner stated. "Now a whole legion of retirees is marching to age sixty-five without a safety net."

The Tax Reform Act didn't even keep our taxes down. Over the last thirteen years the brackets have crept back up, the loopholes have proliferated. A decade after the passage of Bradley's last big idea, during the last presidential election, about 65 percent of the American people told pollsters that the current system was still too complicated and unfair.

Bradley since quit the Senate, getting out while the getting was good. He was right to leave. The senator could never have won reelection. If this is typical of the big ideas Bill Bradley plans to put forward, voters beware.

Now let's take a closer look at some of the more serious fixes being proposed—keeping in mind the need for caution.

THE FLAT TAX

In the coming presidential election you'll hear a lot more about the flat tax. Like a rookie racecar driver who almost won the Indianapolis 500, Steve Forbes rocketed from obscurity to serious-contender status with his flat-tax proposal.

This system would have very few deductions, meaning the middle-class taxpayer would pay the same rate as the richest citizen. At the same time, wealthy people would no longer be able to take advantage of silly tax loopholes (remember that ostrich farm?). Most Americans would supposedly pay the same low, flat, fair rate.

I have a number of objections to the flat tax:

- It is unfair to the poor, eliminating the Earned Income Tax Credit that gives a break to the taxpayers at the lowest rungs of the ladder.

- It is unfair to workers by taxing them for health insurance and other benefits.

- Only the wealthy would reap a windfall, because a flat tax would allow them to cash in interest payments, dividends, and capital gains without paying personal income taxes.

- I don't believe that a flat tax could raise enough revenue to keep the government operating. We would need a higher rate than Steve Forbes proposes in order to get the revenue we need.

My proposal puts the burden on those who can best afford it. A flat tax would give the very wealthy significant additional benefits because they would not be required to pay income taxes on dividends, capital gains, or interest payments.

THE NATIONAL SALES TAX

There is another way to achieve these goals of rewarding savings and extra effort while also making taxes simpler to pay: Replace the federal income and payroll taxes with a national sales tax. If you want to know the true cost of government, you'd find out quickly. You'd pay Uncle Sam directly at the cash register. If nothing else, this tax would be a national eye-opener. Almost everyone would suddenly have a look of pure horror on his or her face.

There are some immediate benefits to this plan. Gone would be the need to fill out numerous forms every year or to keep seven years' worth of financial transactions. And sweetest of all, the IRS would be paired down.

On the downside, we would all pay a lot more for virtually all consumer goods.

THE 10 PERCENT CUT

I'd rather have the people spend the money than have the government spend it. To continue to fund government and public services we could simply reduce tax rates on individuals. This plan, introduced by Republican budget hawk John Kasich of Ohio and Senator Rod Grams of Minnesota, would allow taxpayers who paid income taxes last year at the 15 percent rate to calculate their 1999 taxes at 13.5 percent. Of course, with my debt-reduction plan, the across-the-board cut could be considerably higher than the one proposed by Kasich and Grams.

Until we move to cut tax rates, I would propose other steps that would make our tax laws simpler and fairer.

- One thing we could do now is adopt the Right to Know payroll form. This form would show a clear breakdown of all the hidden taxes paid on your behalf.

- Whatever we decide to do, we should end the marriage penalty.

- We should also repair some recent "fixes," like the Alternative Minimum Tax. When Congress acts to correct its past mistakes, or to make them fairer, the code is so complex that it often leads to "unintended consequences"—a cure that is worse than the disease.

- It is time to go paperless. Nearly 300,000 trees are cut down each year to produce the paper on which IRS forms and instructions are printed. We could save whole forests, and make things easier for taxpayers.

One final point: It's not enough to fix our system of taxation; we also have to look to the other side of the ledger: spending.

Legend has it that it was the Reagan tax cuts that ballooned the deficit in the 1980s. In truth, the tax share in the economy was stabilized by Reagan with his tax cuts and by indexing taxes to inflation. But taxes overall were not reduced. Spending under the old liberal Congress was simply out of control.

Even under a Republican Congress, the government disburses enough pork to make a mile-high ham sandwich. The U.S. public sector is now larger than the entire economy of any country in the world, except Japan.

We need a president who will go to the Congress and tell them what Jesse Ventura told the Minnesota legislature in his State of the State address:

> First, said best by Abraham Lincoln, the role for government is to do only what the people cannot do for themselves. . . . Every time government burdens the people with nonsense like rules that dictate how to butter bread in nursing homes—and believe it or not, that is a real government regulation—we remove any incentive for doing good work. . . .
>
> The State of the State is jeopardized by this weak notion that taxpayers must step forward to provide nearly unlimited resources to anyone who faces adversity . . . who lives with circumstances they brought about through their own decisions . . . or who lives with consequences of choices to act illegally. . . .

America needs to keep a tight rein on spending. Once we eliminate the national debt we need to be careful not to run it up again. We need to reward hard work with a cut in marginal rates. We need to reward savings. We need to make paying taxes easier. And we need a government that gets the point.

"Be fiscally prudent," Governor Ventura says. "Never, ever forget it's the people's money."

Does your presidential candidate remember who's picking up the tab?

★　　　★　　　★

A $5.7 trillion assessment of the extremely wealthy changes the economic landscape. But my proposal would be a one-time event and the only system-wide change I would propose. It would ensure lower rates for working people. It would put our financial house in order and give us time to rethink taxes from the ground up.

CHAPTER SEVEN

Making Social Security Secure Again

T HE FIRST MODERN PYRAMIDS WERE built in Boston in 1919. It all began when hardworking Italian immigrants, chafing at the easy wealth of the blue bloods who dominated their city, were mesmerized by a rumor that some of their neighbors were making vast fortunes from meager savings. The word on the street was that a private firm that called itself the Securities Exchange Company (not to be confused with the Securities and Exchange Commission) was making people rich. Customers, by investing their savings in the SEC's trade in foreign coupons, could make a guaranteed return of 50 percent in little more than a month, and 100 percent in three months.

At such compounded rates, even the humblest ditch digger could become a millionaire within a few years.

As it turns out, the SEC was true to its word. It issued notes and sent notices in the mail inviting customers to cash in their money. Or they could make new investments. The response was overwhelming.

Early in 1920 the SEC was inundated with customers and deposits. With the guarantee of such riches, most customers gleefully redeposited their money. The occasional skeptic who withdrew his account would be rewarded with a full payout at the counter, free advertising that only lured in more customers.

There was a little construction problem, however—one that only the pyramid builders themselves could see.

Despite the rising deposits, coupon investments couldn't begin to allow the SEC to honor the book value of its accounts. Much of the money it did have was spent on other things, such as cars, fancy clothes, and a mansion for the head of the company. The rest of the deposits, which presumably were growing at an annual rate of 400 percent, were piddling along at 5 percent in a local bank.

The managers were men of strong nerves and they flew their Golden Goose through some pretty heavy storms. At one point there was a run on the SEC. When the company began to disburse its obligations in full, confidence was restored. The SEC was back in business, this time taking in $1 million a day. The pyramid grew to great heights.

The day of reckoning finally came in the form of a state investigation. After examining the books of the SEC, Massachusetts's regulators forbade new deposits. That shut off the source of new funds and the SEC pyramid collapsed. Millions of dollars saved from the sweat of working men and women were lost. The thing that looked too good to be true turned out to be exactly that.

The perpetrator of the SEC scheme was none other than Charles Ponzi, whose insight was that if you use Peter to pay Paul, you could create the illusion of vast and growing wealth. Ponzi's story is told by Thomas Streissguth in *Hoaxers & Hustlers*.

Fast-forward to 1941. This is the second year Social Security benefits have been paid. The first recipients of Social Security, even once inflation was factored in, got the equivalent of a 36.5 percent annual interest rate on their initial contributions into the Social Security Trust Fund. For those retiring in 1956, their inflation-adjusted rate of return was still a respectable 12 percent. Julie Kosterlitz, in the *National Journal*, compares that figure with this: For those who are working now and looking to retire after 2015, their returns will be below 2 percent.

And that's if they ever get paid at all.

Does the name Ponzi all of a sudden come to mind?

TALK, NO ACTION

Today Social Security has a liability that's almost $20 trillion. That's roughly $72,700 for every man, woman, and child in the United States. (This figure comes from Senator Robert Kerrey, war hero and Democrat of Nebraska, speaking to the Democratic Leadership Council.) Ink just doesn't get any redder than that.

Yet for years our politicians have made solemn promises to protect Social Security. Perhaps you breathed a sigh of relief when President Clinton said he wants us to save "every dime" of the budget surplus to "save Social Security first!" But if you judge this administration by their deeds, not by their words, you'll see that they've done very little to forestall the day of reckoning.

How can this be?

For the same reason Mr. Ponzi's company was so fantastically behind in meeting its obligations.

"If we began to investigate Social Security, we could become irrationally knowledgeable," writes humorist P. J. O'Rourke. "Our heads might explode. We should not, for example, peek into that Social Security Trust Fund. There's nothing inside."

There is no Social Security Trust Fund any more than there is a tooth fairy. The fund exists only as a bookkeeping device. I repeat: The Social Security Trust Fund, on which scores of millions of Americans base their retirements, is nothing more than a bookkeeping device. (Daniel J. Mitchell has written about this for the Heritage Foundation.) If you went to Washington and demanded that your congressman walk you to the vault and show you this fund, he'd reach under his desk and hit the button to summon the guards. All that exists in the fund is a claim, an IOU on the Treasury that will be honored only if future Congresses honor the obligation of the current and past Congresses.

Economist Milton Friedman, a Nobel Prize winner in economics, characterizes this con game as "balderdash. Taxes paid by today's workers are used to pay today's retirees. If money is left over, it finances other government spending."

To be fair, President Franklin Delano Roosevelt and his labor secretary, Frances Perkins, did not cook up Social Security to defraud the American public. They could not have foreseen four developments that are very much at the heart of the crisis we face.

First, they could not have foreseen that average life expectancy would explode from sixty-one years to seventy-six years today, heading toward eighty years of age by 2030. About 13 percent of our population today is over sixty-five. By 2030 that figure will be more than 20 percent!

Second, FDR and his planners could not have foreseen that retirement would become a lifestyle that would last for a quarter of many people's lives, or longer.

Third, the founders of Social Security could not have foreseen the huge demographic explosion we call the baby boom—a giant bell in the population curve that will land so hard on the Social Security system in the third decade of the twenty-first century that it might crush it.

Fourth and finally, they could not have foreseen family planning.

The pyramid works as long as population steadily increases. As late as 1957, the fertility rate of American women was still high: 3.8 births (that's an average, of course). Today it is 2.0.

As concern about the future rose in the early 1980s, a deal was struck to try to get it back on track. "The law was changed so that Social Security stopped being a pay-as-you-go program," says Kerrey. "Taxes were raised far higher than needed to pay current beneficiaries. Taxes were raised high enough to pre-fund the baby-boom generation. The idea was to build up a several trillion-dollar trust fund that would be gradually drawn down as the baby-boom generation retired.

"Problem was," Kerrey continues, "the promise was broken immediately. Instead of being taxed for the baby boomers, the taxes were used to pay the general bills of government."

This is likely not big news to you. I'm told of one national survey revealing that more Americans under thirty believe in UFOs than believe in the long-term viability of Social Security. In other words, they know they are being lied to about a very important subject. Talk about another reason not to trust government. We always look back to Watergate as the main reason people are suspicious of politicians. Watergate was long ago. The Social Security lie is ongoing.

If you're a young person, you would definitely do better to believe in the *X-Files* than to count on getting your full Social Security benefit.

And even if you do, you'll get it back at a rate of return—below 2 percent—that's half of what you could earn in a savings account in a time of low inflation.

When the first Boomers start to retire after 2013, the program will take in less money in taxes than it owes in benefits. Fortunately, the system is running surpluses invested in treasury notes and can tap the interest earned off these reserves. But by 2021 the Social Security administration will have no choice but to redeem the treasury securities (which are only IOUs) in which the reserves have been "invested."

The current official estimate is that the trust fund will be bankrupt by 2030. If you're age seventy, that might as well be 3020. You're safe. But if you're thirty or forty, you're part of a generation that is in for a world of hurt. You could have made a sounder investment buying lottery tickets.

Social Security actuaries, says Senator Kerrey, project the need for a 25 to 33 percent cut in benefits, or a 25 to 33 percent increase in taxes to maintain benefits for Americans now under the age of forty-five.

The truth is undeniable. The workers of America have been forced to invest a sixth of our wages into a huge Ponzi scheme. The pyramids are made of papier-mâché.

Is there a way out?

LAUNDROMAT ECONOMICS

Yes, there is. There is a way out for us as individuals and as a nation. The way to fiscal national sanity and solvency was pioneered long ago by one Ms. Oseola McCarty.

Ms. McCarty is not your typical economist. In fact she isn't an economist at all. She is a ninety-year-old retired laundry worker from Hattiesburg, Mississippi. Sometimes the best thinking is done in America's laundromats.

For seventy years Oseola labored in a frame house, taking in the dirty clothes of other people and laundering them for a little money. Oseola was thrifty and she managed to save money, enough to invest some of it.

How much did she make? I don't know the full amount, but I have read the news accounts of how she was able to donate $150,000 to provide scholarships for needy students at the University of Southern Mississippi near her home. If you go to that college now you'll find a room set up in Oseola's honor, where her ironing board and washpot are on display. If that doesn't put a lump in your throat, you need a new throat—and a new heart to go with it.

There is a lesson here for the rest of us. A big lesson.

Ms. McCarty long ago realized something that the politicians have not. She understood the wisdom of that old Billy Preston song, "nothing from nothing leaves nothing." She chose to invest her money in something real—an interest-bearing savings account, certificates of deposit, and low-risk mutual funds—and she got something very real in return.

It is likely the mutual funds are the most important in the mix. Since the 1840s the stock market has, over time, outperformed every other investment. Today the stock market promises substantially higher yields than money invested in treasury bonds—7 percent compared with 2.5 percent.

I am the first to sound a note of caution about the stock market. I agree with Federal Reserve Board Chairman Alan Greenspan that there's a great deal of "irrational exuberance" out there. The gains of the kinds the markets have been posting in these last five years cannot be sustained. As I explained in other chapters, we could face a crash, or at least a correction, that will knock the fillings out of some very pretty teeth.

I give the same advice to people who have an economic cushion. When Mike Tyson was making $50 to $100 million a year from his amazing success in the ring, I advised him to put his money in a solid bank and in treasury bills. Mike was careless with money; he wasn't much interested in it. More speculative investment would have been risky for him.

But stocks aren't the only place to invest. Social Security money could be invested in REITS—real estate portfolios run by professional managers. Or it could be invested in bonds, which typically offer a lower yield but less risk than stocks. Or better yet, all of the above.

In a country where politicians, economists, and other professional nags are always telling us that we Americans don't save enough, doesn't it make sense for us to save our Social Security dollars—I mean really save them—in the productive assets of our country?

The solution to the Great Social Security Crisis couldn't be more obvious: Allow every American to dedicate some portion of their payroll taxes to a personal Social Security account that they could own and invest in stocks and bonds. Federal guidelines could make sure that your money is diversified, that it is invested in sound mutual funds or bond funds, and not in emu ranches.

The national savings rate would soar and billions of dollars would be cycled from savings, to productive assets, to retirement money. And unlike the previous system, the assets in this retirement account could be left to one's heirs, used to start a business, or anything else one desires.

This sounds simple, so simple that it takes a ninety-year-old retired washerwoman to make plain a solution that has eluded politicians and economists from the elite universities.

The strength of the idea, letting people keep the money that is rightfully theirs and investing in something more valuable than IOUs, is gaining so much popularity that the politicians are being forced to pay lip service to it.

READ THE LABEL

But be careful of substitutes. There are a number of plans that sound similar, but . . .

President Clinton, for example, is proposing that Social Security funds be invested on your behalf by federal bureaucrats. This would give you no say in how your money is invested. And it would effectively put Uncle Sam in the boardroom of every major corporation in America—an eight-hundred-pound gorilla of a shareholder no company could ignore.

When Federal Chairman Alan Greenspan was asked about Clinton's plan, he said it "has very far-reaching potential dangers for a free American economy and a free American society."

To see why, you need only look to the states. State pension fund managers routinely throw around their financial weight, intervening in the private sector.

If Social Security is invested in the markets by government, Uncle Sam will use its power to force companies not to do business in unfashionable countries or industries. It will also have the power to strong-arm companies involved in labor or environmental disputes. It will have the power to advance politically correct cronies to run companies the way Washington wants them run.

We can get a better idea of how this plan would work by considering just who has the big pull in Washington. Big tobacco, for instance, pumps lots of money into politics and still has a lot of friends. So does the NRA. A lot of people aren't going to want their tax dollars thrown into stocks that help these groups. Let me hit a little closer to home. There's no doubt that the casino industry has pretty good political pull. Lots of people, however, aren't big on gambling and wouldn't want the government to be helping that industry any more than it already does. The fact is, if we let the political class decide where all these billions go, we will have made lobbyists the new masters of the universe.

This is the ultimate nightmare, a fusion of big government and big business. And it's a nightmare with teeth. Public investment of Social Security funds would import to America an Asian-style crony capitalism—the very cause of the recent collapse in economies from Seoul to Singapore.

Okay, so Clinton's plan is worse than no plan at all. What then should we do?

For the short term, Americans should support the Republican proposal to put Social Security in a "lock box" says Representative James Rogan, a Republican from California.

This proposal is ingenious for its simplicity. It would end the practice of the general treasury spending Social Security surpluses. This lock-box proposal would require two-thirds approval from Congress to use any of the $1.8 trillion in projected Social Security surpluses over the next decade for anything other than Social Security or Medicare.

"That's a high threshold to make sure we spend those dollars [only] on real emergencies," Rogan says, and adds a swipe at the Democrats. "On their forty-year watch, not one dime was locked away. They spent that trust fund like a drunken sailor on shore leave."

The White House, it should come as no surprise, strongly opposes the lock-box idea and is out to block it. The president is still on shore leave, it appears.

The GOP comes up with some pretty stupid stuff of its own, of course. Congress dipped into the trust fund this spring to meet President Clinton's request for a bill that took $15 billion in "emergency" spending. The package included almost twice what Clinton requested to finance air strikes in Yugoslavia, and larded on a bunch of pork spending to boot.

I say it is high time to separate Social Security from the general treasury. It is time to lock-box it and throw away the key.

WORKING SENIORS

Another relatively easy thing we can do is stop penalizing retirement-age seniors for working. This won't directly help to save Social Security, but it will go a long way toward restoring fairness to the system. More than that, the very idea of penalizing someone for working is *the* dumbest idea ever to come out of Washington. I know the competition is stiff, but I believe that idea wins the blue ribbon.

If you're a poor working senior between sixty-five and sixty-nine, and you want to supplement your Social Security by working, the government will heap a 33.3 percent disincentive on you not to work. Add this to your federal, state, and local tax burden, and you can see that the low-income elderly who work are paying an effective tax rate that is as high as 65 percent!

Fortunately, Senator John McCain of Arizona was successful in passing a bill to gradually raise the Social Security earnings limit. I think it's now time to scrap it altogether.

We can also raise the age for receipt of full Social Security benefits to seventy.

This proposal would not include anyone who is currently retired or about to retire. Don't put your water skis back in the basement; it would be set for those who would retire well into the third or fourth decade of the twenty-first century.

A firm limit at age seventy makes sense for people now under forty. We're living longer. We're working longer. New medicines are extending healthy human life. Besides, how many times will you really want to take that trailer to the Grand Canyon? The way the workweek is going, it will probably be down to about twenty-five hours by then anyway. This is a sacrifice I think we all can make. And I don't accept the criticism that it's easy for guys like me to tell thirty-year-olds they shouldn't retire until they're seventy. Like a lot of people I know, I plan to work forever. My father was in his late eighties before he stopped coming to the office. If you're wondering when my retirement date will be, it will be about one day shy of the death date chiseled on my tombstone.

Finally, we have to allow individuals to invest some portion of their Social Security funds in investments that are real and conservative, just like Oseola McCarty did. And we must allow individuals to leave this nest egg to their heirs—just as Ms. McCarty did.

Democrats have good proposals of their own.

Senators Daniel Patrick Moynihan and Bob Kerrey are advancing a proposal to cut payroll taxes by $800 over the next ten years and shift this tax revenue into individual wealth accounts that would be owned by beneficiaries. When Democrats talk about tax cuts, it's our national duty to jump in behind them. Let me be the first in line.

Privatization would be good for all of us. As it stands today, 13.6 percent of women on Social Security live in poverty. Harvard University researchers studied almost two thousand American women who retired in 1981 and found that virtually every woman—single, divorced, married, or widowed—would probably be better off financially under a system of fully private investment accounts. Not one woman would have been worse off. On average, personal accounts would have provided a single woman with 58 percent more than Social Security, and wives with 208 percent more.

Directing Social Security funds into personal accounts invested in real assets would swell national savings, pumping hundreds of billions of dollars into jobs and the economy. These investments would boost national investment, productivity, wages, and future economic growth.

Washington will probably put off doing anything about Social Security until after the 2000 election. That means it will be 2002 at the earliest before you can expect to be allowed to invest some of your own Social Security money. According to David Broder, the respected political reporter for the *Washington Post*:

> [B]oth parties have decided that short-term political risks
> and rewards count more than long-term solutions. But as the
> window closes, I can't help but wonder if a door has opened
> for an independent or third-party candidate in 2000 who can
> say to the millions of young families surrendering large por-
> tions of every paycheck to taxes for Social Security and
> Medicare benefits that few of them believe they will ever
> receive. . . . The Republicans and Democrats have demon-
> strated they lack the courage and the will to help you. If you
> want something done about this, you have to find someone
> else to support—someone who is not tied to, or terrified by,
> the interest groups supporting the status quo.

★   ★   ★

That candidate likely won't be Ross Perot or Jesse Ventura. But the opening is there.

If my reading of the public mood is right, the younger voters espe-cially are ready for some straight shooting about Social Security. They know that Social Security, unless reformed, is going to collapse on their heads. These younger voters are the natural constituency of Jesse Ventura and a handful of others. America's elected officials must have the courage to take on this problem in a bipartisan way. The growing divide between the rich and the poor in this country shouldn't strand seniors on the far side. Check your candidates. Are they playing polit-ical football or are they making a run for the American Dream?

CHAPTER EIGHT

To Our Health

W E USED TO COMPLAIN, HALF JOKINGLY, that doctors didn't make house calls anymore. Today many Americans can't even get in their doctors' doors for the medical attention they need. It has become difficult to get and pay for a doctor to cure us or to keep us well. And there's nothing funny about that at all.

HMOs and PPOs aren't working. Prescription medicine is hard to come by at a reasonable price. Medicare is suffering from immense financing problems.

This breakdown in doctor-patient relations is caused by the growth of a new bureaucracy—the health insurance delivery system. Whether through managed care, fee-for-service, Medicare, or other types of health coverage, many decisions are being made by people whose primary qualification is that they can type quickly and handle phone calls.

It is infuriating that this malfunctioning bureaucracy is endangering lives. American healthcare has a couple of toes in the grave despite the fact that our medical science is the most advanced on earth. When a sheik or a king rubs his belly and discovers a troubling lump, it is highly unlikely that he'll board his personal jet and fly to a country with socialized medicine. Far from it. He'll fly straight to the Mayo Clinic. In fact just about anyone who can afford to come to the United States for healthcare will do so. And yet top-of-the-line American medical science is out of reach of most Americans.

The healthcare bureaucrats are depriving Americans of care in order to keep costs down. Medical care is so expensive, in fact, that millions of Americans have no health insurance at all.

Here's the real scandal: According to James Frogue in a Heritage Foundation memorandum, around ten million American children have no insurance coverage. This isn't to say they can't get medical attention—though some activists would have us think so—but they are often treated in hospital emergency rooms, which is the most expensive type of care. Routine medical care for these kids often doesn't exist.

Nor are things any better for the elderly. In general, whatever is wrong with healthcare is even more so for Medicare. If you are worried about the future of Social Security—as you definitely should be—then you should be frantic about the future of Medicare, because we are already experiencing some of the funding problems with Medicare that we fear might happen with Social Security in a couple of decades.

The structure of the healthcare industry is confusing and expensive at every level, and there's no simple solution. Since the Truman administration our country has been trying to implement a system that protects all citizens.

I'm a conservative on most issues but a liberal on this one. We should not hear so many stories of families ruined by healthcare expenses. We must not allow citizens with medical problems to go untreated because of financial problems or red tape. It is an unacceptable but accurate fact that the number of uninsured Americans has risen to forty-two million.

Working out detailed plans will take time. But the goal should be clear: Our people are our greatest asset. We must take care of our own. We must have universal healthcare.

Just imagine the improved quality of life for our society as a whole if the issue of access to healthcare were dealt with imaginatively. With more than forty million Americans living day to day in the fear that an illness or injury will wipe out their savings or drag them into bankruptcy, how can we truly engage in the "pursuit of happiness" as our Founders intended?

UNIVERSAL CARE

What would universal care look like?

Nebraska senator Kerrey and others have advocated a version of the Canadian-style, single-payer system in which all payments for medical care are made to a single agency (as opposed to the large number of HMOs and insurance companies, with their diverse rules, claim forms, and deductibles). A recent study done by the Massachusetts Medical Society says that in Massachusetts the single-payer plan would save $5 billion or about one-seventh of the overhead spent on medical care. Administrative costs across America make up 25 percent of the healthcare dollar, which is two-and-a-half times the cost of healthcare administration in Canada. Doctors might be paid less than they are now, as is the case in Canada, but they would be able to treat more patients because of the reduction in their paperwork.

The Canadian plan also helps Canadians live longer and healthier than Americans. There are fewer medical lawsuits, less loss of labor to sickness, and lower costs to companies paying for the medical care of their employees. If the program were in place in Massachusetts in 1999 it would have reduced administrative costs by $2.5 million.

We need, as a nation, to reexamine the single-payer plan, as many individual states are doing.

But implementing such a plan is not simple. One major problem is that the single-payer plan in Canada is in financial difficulty, as is the nationalized plan in the United Kingdom. We have to improve on the prototype.

PHASE ONE: HEALTH AND TAXES

History makes it obvious that it will take several years to revamp the healthcare system from the bottom up. While we work out details of a new single-payer plan, there are a number of ways to make the health-care system now in place work more efficiently.

As things stand now, most people rely on their employers for healthcare coverage. They are obviously thankful for those health benefits, but there are problems with this approach. Employers own the policies provided and determine what the benefits are, and usually it's a one-size-fits-all situation. The people actually covered by the policies have little if any input in how the policy is structured. In this age of managed care, that puts an enormous segment of our population at the mercy of a large and increasingly impersonal health industry— one that too often puts the bottom line first, and curing you and your family second.

For starters, we need to find a better way to fund medical care.

Let's begin by looking at tax reform.

The way the system works now, businesses that provide coverage for their employees get a significant tax break because the cost of health-care benefits is a tax-deductible expense. The cost of healthcare benefits is also a tax exclusion from the employees' income and payroll taxes.

We need a change in the tax code that would give groups and individuals tax breaks for health insurance that are equivalent to those that corporations now receive. This would allow ordinary citizens to buy coverage that complements their company policy and gives them more of what they need. It would also give them the option to jettison the company policy altogether and just buy their own insurance. Low-income families would also benefit greatly from tax credits that they could use to buy insurance or to pay for medical care directly. Community groups other than employers—unions and churches, for example—should also be allowed the same tax break as employers.

Reform of the tax code should help level the healthcare playing field for uninsured Americans. Since the average healthcare plan would cost around $3,000, we should also explore providing a refundable tax credit of about that amount for any family that can't get private health insurance through work or through an existing government program.

We don't want to remove the incentive for employers to continue to provide health insurance benefits. Therefore we'd need to fine-tune the tax-credit program.

CHOICE
The system also needs more flexibility. Because different families need different kinds of healthcare coverage, there is a distinct need to build choice into the delivery system

Surgeon General Everett Koop, who is always worth listening to, wrote recently that, "The days of the authoritative physician and the passive patient are gone. . . . Ultimately, you are the one who holds the keys to getting the best your health system has to offer." Unfortunately, many of us have little or no choice in what we're covered for.

It wasn't that long ago that the idea of choice in medicine would have seemed radical if not crazy. When my parents were young, you went to the doctor (or he came to you), you got his advice, and you did what you were told. Doctors were trained to believe in the infallibility of their diagnosis and treatment, and we took them at their word.

As if in response to the democratizing of medicine, the network of doctors, hospitals, pharmaceutical companies, and insurance companies expanded and grew tighter. Whether you wanted one or not, a second opinion was offered by an insurance adjuster or a healthcare maintenance provider. And that's where we stand today. People are being restrained from getting the medical attention they need because an army of bureaucrats is looking over doctors' shoulders and telling them what to do.

The health insurance system is a vestige of another era, one in which there were three television channels, two kinds of coffee (with or without cream), and one kind of bread (white). Most people have little choice and shrinking benefits in medical insurance. We insist on two hundred cable channels and thirty types of coffee at the local kiosk, but we put up with these very limited options in health coverage.

ADMINISTRATION

Let's go back and look at the medical bureaucracy I was talking about. There may have been reasons once upon a time for medical-care review.

It prevented cost overruns and abuse. America is a generous country but also a country that believes in fairness. We don't like tax cheats, welfare cheats, or medical cheats. And so we used to put up with the growth of the healthcare bureaucracy because we thought it would prevent the system from being overburdened and misused.

And then somebody began to analyze costs.

Just recently the United Health Group, one of our biggest managed-care companies, said it was returning decision-making power for treatment of illness to doctors themselves. They retain the right to say that the price of a medical procedure is too high, but they will do what the doctor recommends.

Is this a crazy decision? Doesn't it mean that all sorts of unnecessary medicine will be practiced? Apparently a lot of people don't think so. Physicians, consumer groups, and President Clinton welcomed the change. The price of United stock even advanced a small amount.

Why did United make such an extraordinary change in the way they operate? They discovered that they were approving 99 percent of the requested procedures. The company will save about $100 million by phasing out its review procedure. If this change is made by other insurers it means that we may be about to enter an era in which patients and doctors will be better satisfied and in which there may even be more choice.

EMERGENCY REPAIRS

Short term, there are a few more small improvements to existing care that we can accomplish right now.

We can do more for children of uninsured families. By giving their parents assistance in buying the family's policy, we can put these kids into a stable situation in which they have a doctor who knows them by name, not one who, by necessity, is doing assembly-line medicine.

Congress took a few timid steps to subsidize health insurance for some poor children in 1997, but too many kids are still falling through the cracks. There are countless stories of moms and dads refusing to let their kids ride bikes, skateboards, or play after-school sports because they lack insurance and one injury would be too costly for the family to afford. Health and fitness go hand in hand for our kids. Let's get them covered so they can blossom physically and so we can give peace of mind to their hard-working parents.

There are many other ingenious, smaller fixes we should consider. Some analysts are pushing the idea of health marts, which would treat private-sector employees much like public-sector people. Health marts would create a group of approved plans for employees or independents to select from. This would give them control over their healthcare decisions.

We're already seeing some employees banding together in order to purchase insurance as a group. There is, for instance, the Buyers' Healthcare Action Group in Minneapolis, which was formed by workers who didn't like their at-work policies.

For individuals, Flexible Spending Accounts and Medical Savings Accounts give greater flexibility in healthcare purchasing. FSAs are tax-free accounts into which workers designate a portion of the money for emergencies or benefits not covered in employer-based programs. Their employers can also contribute. MSAs are an alternative to group health insurance and managed care. Both individuals and employers may make contributions to these accounts.

But there are downsides to these programs that need to be corrected. FSAs have use-it-or-lose-it provisions. If you don't use your funds during the year, they will be forfeited back to the employer. This gives participants a considerable incentive to spend on marginally beneficial care. Congress has allowed a few people and some small businesses to open MSAs with a rollover provision. This policy needs to be expanded.

KEEPING MEDICARE AFLOAT

I own my own company and make my own deals with health providers. But I can relate to the problems of medical care for the elderly. My mother, Mary, has osteoporosis. She's broken bones something like two hundred times in her life and is now wheelchair-bound. No, she doesn't have to worry about the cost of healthcare; we can give her the best. But she damn well cares about the quality of medical attention she gets. And so do I.

Some fundamental questions about Medicare are not financial but qualitative: Will the next generation of Medicare patients be able to choose the kinds of plans, benefits, and medical treatments they want? Will they be free of bureaucratic restrictions on their personal choices? Will they be protected from arrogant invasions of medical privacy?

Although the healthcare system is privatized and Medicare is run by a single government agency, the problems are the same: too little choice for consumers, too few funds with which to operate. Under current law, Medicare's hospitalization benefits are paid out of the Hospital Insurance (HI) Trust Fund. According to current projections reported by Robert E. Moffit for the Heritage Foundation, the HI fund faces insolvency by 2015. But we don't have to wait until then for the problems. They're already here.

The U.S. government's General Accounting Office, an objective investigative arm of the Congress, paints an ugly picture:

Unlike Social Security, Medicare's HI program has been experiencing a cash-flow deficit since 1992—current payroll taxes and other revenues have been insufficient to cover benefit payments and program expenses. . . . In essence, Medicare has already crossed the point where it is a net claimant on the Treasury—a threshold that Social Security is not expected to reach until 2013. . . .

The current Medicare program is both economically and fiscally unsustainable. This is not a new message—the Medicare trustees noted in the early 1990s that the program is unsustainable in its present form.

So why aren't we engaged in a full-fledged effort to reform Medicare? One reason is that healthcare costs have been held relatively low over the past couple of years and this gives us a false sense of security. Very false in fact. Combined with Social Security, medical-program costs are quickly becoming a malignancy in the heart of the Treasury.

The other reason we haven't explored changes is that it takes a lot of political guts to talk about taking the steps we need to take to put the system on sounder footing. Medicare administers to elderly people on small fixed incomes. Rock the boat even a little and, understandably, they get nervous. But the longer we wait the worse the illness gets.

We need to work hard to keep Medicare solvent. While we do that, we also have to change the Medicare culture to one that offers the diversity of coverage our senior citizens deserve.

Many Medicare reforms have been floated, but they have been, for the most part, meaningless. This includes President Clinton's plan in early

1999, which the GAO blasted. It's instructive to look closer at Clinton's response to the crisis, because it was a perfect illustration of the typical political response to the Medicare crisis.

The president proposed to pump in a hefty financial transfusion: 15 percent of the projected budget surplus—$700 billion—over the next fifteen years. This would allegedly keep HI funded until 2020. At first this looked pretty good. Yet, as the GAO pointed out, this money would otherwise be used to pay off national debt, so the gain to taxpayers is exactly nil. And that was the least of this plan's problems.

Clinton stared at the beast—and blinked. He chose to avoid the hard decisions that will have to be made down the road where, as the GAO points out, they will be much more painful.

But let's face it, Clinton is hardly the only politician to duck a tough issue. It will take a new breed of politician to push meaningful reform. It requires a risk-taker with titanium nerves and vision.

The fact is, painful or not, we won't be able to put Medicare on firmer footing until we insist that beneficiaries carry more of the burden. Now that we enjoy longer life expectancy we will have to move the Medicare eligibility age to seventy, which reflects the trend toward a longer stay in the workplace by millions of Americans. And we'll have to take on the lobbyists and interest groups that want to keep the system pretty much the way it is because they are profiting from it.

LONG-TERM CARE

There's one more aspect of the medical-insurance story that is almost totally off the typical radar screen. This one involves long-term care. With the baby-boom generation heading toward retirement and their parents already there, this is a huge issue.

A few numbers tell the story: The number of elderly will double to seventy-seven million by 2030 and the number of seniors in nursing homes will increase fivefold.

I know the response: Doesn't Medicaid pay for nursing homes? This question is often asked by Boomers who figure their parents will be covered, as will they when their time comes to book some long-term care.

Here's the answer: Medicaid was never meant to be a long-term-care provider. And as Senator John Breaux and Representative William Thomas have pointed out, "The growing demand for long-term care is pushing the Medicaid program into bankruptcy."

Nearly one in two Americans will need some type of long-term care but only one in four can afford long-term private nursing-home care, which now averages around $41,000 a year. Only 1 percent of Americans has bought long-term healthcare insurance. So most are hoping to rely on Medicaid. As things are right now, they're in for a major disappointment.

After a short initial contribution, Medicaid will drop out of the picture until the patient's resources are spent down to the poverty level. If the patients are your parents, that means everything they've worked for in life will be gone. And that often means one parent is left destitute. It can also create a massive financial burden on families. The Boomer who had planned to sail around the world on his own boat might find himself selling his car to keep mom or dad in a decent facility.

What can we do about this?

This is a case where a strong private-public effort is necessary. Until a better plan is in place, we need to encourage those who can afford long-term insurance to buy it. Those who can't afford it will have to rely on public subsidies. Government can offer some tax incentives here for policy buyers. More than anything else, at least for now, we must make Americans understand that they are not covered the way most believe they are.

We must also encourage insurance companies to offer more diversity in their plans. The Health Insurance Association reports that while there are around one thousand insurance companies operating in the U.S., the vast majority—over 80 percent—of long-term-care policies has been written by eleven of those companies.

There is a huge crisis in care just over the hill. According to one insurance estimate, one out of every five Americans over the age of fifty will need long-term care within a year. Yet almost everyone is uninsured. If you can afford long-term-care insurance and don't buy it, you probably need to rethink your life—before you end up in a nursing home without such a policy.

THE PACE OF REFORM

Though we need to make radical improvements, we must not try to go too swiftly in reinventing the system. Rule number one: Take a lesson from Hillary Clinton's attempt to "fix" the healthcare system.

No one can deny her good intentions. Clinton's was the first administration in years with the ambition to try to help healthcare. But Mrs. Clinton was and is politically committed to a world view that would have done for modern American medicine what Joseph Stalin did for Ukrainian agriculture.

We don't want more government control of the healthcare industry, which is what the Clinton plan called for. There's more than just a little of the den mother at work here. Hillary Clinton thought she knew best, but her plan would likely have created huge bureaucratic night-mares and inefficiencies.

THE CURE

So our objective is to make reforms for the moment and, longer term, to find an equivalent of the single-payer plan that is affordable, well administered, and provides freedom of choice.

Possible? The good news is, yes. There is already a system in place—the Federal Employees Health Benefits Program—that can act as a guide for all healthcare reform. It operates through a centralized agency that offers considerable range of choice. While this is a government program, it is also very much market based. It allows 620 private insurance companies to compete for this market. Once a year the participants can choose from up to two dozen different plans, which vary in benefits and costs. The 1998 *Candidate's Briefing Book* says that this is about the only system that allows families so much variety in their healthcare.

The government manages this plan with a light hand through the Office of Personnel Management. Its role is limited but precise. Each spring, health providers are asked to submit proposals for their plans, stating benefits and costs. After the proposals come in, the Office of Personnel Management negotiates with the providers. This allows for competition and gives federal workers an excellent range of options.

Medicare could certainly be operated the same way; a single-payer, universal plan ought to be as well.

Borrowing from the Federal Employees Health Benefits Program model, there would be real competition within the insurance market-place to develop a package of benefits attractive to the eligible families.

There would be countless economic benefits from improved access to healthcare—such as fewer missed days of work and fewer financial losses for hospitals and doctors who provide services without compensation. Further, it would reduce the burden on other governmental programs that deal with the health problems facing uninsured children and adults.

Following Stuart M. Butler in a Heritage Foundation backgrounder, here's how I would re-create the Federal Benefits model for the whole country.

I would immediately create a board to set rules for providers and also to negotiate with them. This board would establish firm rules that ensure seniors a solid core of benefits. It would also include more options for higher levels of service. The seniors' contributions would be adjusted according to income and need level. "Premium support" services would be more limited, which would give them an incentive to find the most cost-effective base plan.

At the same time I would create a board to oversee benefits changes in a nonpartisan setting. To ensure independence for consumers, we need an independent board to set the rules and to make sure that all parties live up to them. Our priority must be our citizens, not our lobbyists.

★   ★   ★

My critics will say that Trump, uncharacteristically, puts too much faith in bureaucracy; a single-payer plan would create a gigantic agency to distribute funds to doctors. I'd point out that by creating one agency we do away with hundreds of smaller ones that are hard to monitor.

My critics may also say that Trump puts too much faith in the American public. He believes they are capable of choosing from among a wide array of healthcare options. He believes they are intelligent and sophisticated enough to choose more wisely than the experts can choose for them.

Exactly. I do believe that, just as I believe Americans are ready, willing, and able to take control of their own retirement accounts. And their children's education. And their streets. And their tax system. And every other aspect of public life that has been commandeered by the governing elite.

But I don't believe this will happen until we make freedom possible. We do that by finding politicians gutsy enough to make these issues their issues.

CHAPTER NINE

The Politics We Deserve

ONEY AND POLITICS — NOW THERE'S a pair of ugly twins. In fact it doesn't get much uglier. I've seen beggars in the streets with more dignity than some politicians on the hunt for a handout. The panhandlers make no pretensions about what they're up to. They'll take your buck and exchange it for a beer or use it as a down payment on a bottle of rotgut. It's a clean transaction.

But the political pro tells you your donation will go toward the defense of mom, apple pie, chastity, charity, Bambi, truth, justice, virtue, and to ensure that the sun continues to rise in the East and set in the West. They tell you this with a straight face. We all know better, of course. Money is job security for a politician. What he's really saying is, "Please help me keep my job, otherwise I'll have to go back to work at my father-in-law's furniture showroom."

I am forever amused and amazed at the lengths to which politicians will go for a donation. They'll kiss babies, grandmothers, your pet iguana—whatever it takes. They'll go buck-raking through

Buddhist temples, pig-pickings, bass tournaments, roller derbies, Red China, and anyplace else where there's the slightest possibility that a guy will scratch them a check.

Most will tell you whatever they think you want to hear. There's an old joke: Never sit down too fast at a political fundraiser, because you might break the guest of honor's nose. They'll also pick up the phone and call perfect strangers. Sometimes those calls come from the county commissioner's office; sometimes they come from the White House.

Despite the indignities, crudities, and sometime complete outrageousness of political fundraising, we still have a pretty good political system. Roughly speaking, it succeeds in producing representatives who respond to public desires. It weeds out the cranks and flakes—most of the time anyway. And despite a few truly bad apples, we get a pretty good field of candidates and we also elect some very good public servants. When the inclination toward cynicism grows powerful, we need to keep this in mind.

But we could do better.

There's no doubt that we can improve the way that we finance elections. Many Americans, myself included, believe the system isn't working as well as it could. We believe it is too beholden to special interests, which it is. And there is a general belief that the regular citizen who bothers to participate in the process is not being heard as loudly and clearly as should be the case. If they're not drowned out by unions, corporations, and lobbyists, they find themselves playing second fiddle to Chinese gardeners and other foreign-money mules.

So change is needed. But not just any change. All most Americans want is a financing system that reflects our bedrock values—it should be fair, just, honest, and heavily tilted in the direction of individual rights.

Campaign reform up until now has tried to clean up the system by controlling the inflow of money. It limited contributions by individuals and corporations; it attempted to use public money to finance elections. The system limited the size of donations to an absurdly low figure that encouraged contributors to open up loopholes big enough to drive a tank through.

What's wrong with this approach is what's wrong with all regulation: It limits personal freedom, it can't be enforced, and it can always be evaded.

Campaign finance doesn't need to be made stricter. All the regulations so far have failed to address the problem. Political contributors don't corrupt the system by giving too much. They corrupt the system by being able to act *in secret*. If a strip-mining company gives a million dollars to Senator X in hopes he'll vote against a sweeping environmental protection law, nobody will be surprised. That company ought to have the right to do whatever it can to improve business. If you limit the strip miner to a tiny donation he'll find some way around the law.

The way to fix American politics is not to limit donations but to make sure that those donations and the donor are on the public record.

So my proposals for campaign reform will seem groundbreaking to many of you. Nevertheless, I'm convinced that they are the only way to correct the abuses.

Let's look at some fundamental facts about our political system. We have a representative democracy and, if you want your views represented, you find the right candidate and work for him or her. That might mean going door to door. That might mean sticking up a yard sign. That might mean manning a booth outside a polling place or standing on a street corner on election day waving a flag and blowing a horn. People do funny things around election time, but it's part of the democratic pageant. Some may laugh at them, but the core fact is that these people care about where this country is heading and they know we aren't going to get there on automatic pilot.

Engaging in politics might also mean supporting your candidate with a donation. In this age of media-driven campaigns, candidates are especially receptive to a check, and the bigger the better. Money has always been the mother's milk of politics, but these days you need an extraordinary amount of milk to keep a campaign afloat. Television advertising is very expensive and if you can't afford it you had better stick to your day job.

I think a lot of people were probably astounded to learn that President Clinton was so personally involved in the creation of media messages in his most recent presidential campaign—one that relied on some pretty sleazy funding tricks, as we now know—that he apparently wrote some of the advertising messages himself.

Americans assume that a president has better things to do than write ad copy, but in a game where image counts for so much, it really isn't surprising to see even the leader of the most powerful country in the world being involved at this level. And as we saw in this particular campaign, the president—and his Republican challenger as well—were so desperate for ad money that they clearly abused party funds, channeling them directly into their war chests and violating the spirit of the law and probably the letter of the law also. They took money wherever they could find it. They also personally worked the phones—in the president's case, once again in a way that raised legal questions. Sometimes they went overseas, which to my mind raises questions that are a lot more troubling.

KEEPING THE PEOPLE IN CHARGE

How do we cut out the excesses without putting the government at the heart of the funding process? How can we make sure the little guy is not drowned out by the corporate CEO? How can we make sure the unions don't drown out the voices of millions of unorganized but equally passionate voters?

These are questions as old as our democracy. But they have taken on an increased urgency as we've seen the cost of campaigns go through the roof. The pressure to raise money threatens to make politics strictly a game for big givers—mainly corporations and unions—leaving the little guy as a mere observer, if he doesn't walk away altogether.

The good news is that it would not be hard to give Americans the system they desire and deserve. In fact it would be simple.

Goal one: Make sure that individual Americans are allowed to support their candidates to the fullest degree they desire. Political participation should be considered one of the highest uses of the First Amendment's free-speech guarantee. This right should be all but absolute, as are other free-speech rights. That way we empower each individual, assuring him or her that they can fly as high in this game as their talents will take them—not merely as high as a panel of bureaucrats allows.

Having freed the individual from restraints on his or her ability to support a candidate, we move to goal two: Make sure that the big boys—especially corporations and unions—do not overpower the system with those unlimited donations known as "soft money."

A few finance reforms are better than others. Some are positively malignant. At the top of the list is financing campaigns purely through public funding—that is, with tax money. This is wrong for a couple of reasons. As the Founders pointed out, there is one word to describe the act of forcing citizens to support a person or cause they reject: tyranny.

And that is exactly what public funding would create. Let me give you an example. A lot of my intelligent and enlightened friends believe that public funding would take the corruption out of politics. They believe it would put citizens on an equal basis with corporate CEOs (they don't usually add union bosses, so I'll do that for them). In short, they believe government regulation would put the unruly political pack in order and everything would be fine. They haven't gotten the word yet that if something is partially botched and you want to totally screw up the job, bring in the government.

I say to these people: So you're in favor of having your tax dollars automatically pumped into Pat Buchanan's campaign chest? And if David Duke makes a strong run down South you'd be happy to support him too? All of a sudden the lights go on and the smiles leave their faces. And you can turn my examples around. Why should a deeply conservative person in the Midwest, who works his or her fingers to the bone in a tough, unforgiving job, be forced to financially support a liberal candidate whose agenda is a total rejection of this person's belief system?

The answer is that they shouldn't. Sure, if people want to check off the public funding box on their tax returns, that's their business.

But forced public funding of the entire political process is wrong, and not only because it forces us to support those we abhor. Over the years I've contributed about equally to both parties.

In an earlier chapter I argued that the government shouldn't be allowed to invest Social Security funds in the stock market. Why? Because we should not let the federal government become the central player in any market—financial, political, or otherwise. In fact the very idea of candidates being funded by the government that they hope to join is entirely incestuous.

Public funding is a bad idea and so is a similarly strong-armed measure that would force television stations to give "free" airtime to candidates. I put free in quotation marks because the entire concept is bogus. There's nothing free about it. Candidates might get on the air for free, but the paying customers will in one way or another pick up the slack.

I don't like the idea of the federal government informing media companies that they must run a certain type of programming. It all has a strong whiff of dictatorship about it. I'm shocked that this idea has gained currency among journalists, a couple of whom have been foremost in the drive for forced advertising. Some people get the night sweats whenever a city council goes behind closed doors or whenever a petty official tells a camera crew to back off, but they turn around and support laws that would force television networks to air commercials for people running for high office.

As I said about healthcare, we fix our system by electing the right people to office. And we elect the right people by cleaning up the election process.

How?

First I want to take on the special interests. These are fat targets, and if I were drawing a political cartoon to represent the situation it would include a very large guy with a huge bag of money. On that bag would be written one word: *soft*. Soft money is the bane of the current system and we need to get rid of it.

SOFT MONEY, HARD EDGE

What precisely is soft money? It is unlimited money given to political parties that is not supposed to find its way into the war chests of specific national candidates. Of course it does find its way into those war chests, often at very delicate times.

The public-interest group Common Cause, an organization that is respected across the board for its abilities to track soft money, has a good definition of what the soft-money phenomenon is all about. It was "developed in recent years to provide candidates, contributors, and political parties a means to evade federal contribution limits and source prohibitions." In other words, soft money is a huge legal sham. It is in complete contradiction to the existing law. (You can check these statistics yourself at the Common Cause Web site: www.commoncause.org.)

Soft money is a creation of the Federal Election Commission. It came into being in 1978 but wasn't really exploited until the 1988 presidential campaign. Now it's out of control. "Soft money exploded from $86 million in the 1992 election to $260 million in 1996, and it could well triple again to $750 million for the presidential campaign in the year 2000," says Common Cause.

Remember my earlier warning about who would have the greatest say in how Social Security funds would be invested in the stock market? If you want to see precisely who would pull those strings, look at the people who give the big soft-money contributions. The securities and investments industry gives the most to the Republicans ($9,077,625 during the most recent election cycle). The insurance industry gave $8,596,882 and the oil and gas industry gave $6,004,861. All could definitely benefit directly from government stock investment, and you can be assured they would twist the appropriate arms until they got what they wanted.

Meanwhile, unions gave $9,965,667 to Democrats in 1997–1998—making organized labor the largest soft-money supplier to that party. Lawyers and lobbyists gave $6,533,150, and securities and investments interests gave $6,268,802. Trial lawyers squeeze lots of money out of legitimate enterprises as it is. Does anyone really believe they wouldn't put the squeeze on the people who so readily accept their donations?

Soft money goes to the parties, who turn around and spend it on activities and schemes to help get their candidate elected. This often comes in the form of "issues" advertising, which is in itself a loophole. These ads supposedly speak only to issues. They are not supposed to directly benefit or harm a candidate.

But these ads are a total joke, at least regarding their adherence to the law. They leave no doubt who is being supported and who is being attacked.

Most people who are involved in politics are good-hearted citizens who care deeply for our country. While most of us are sleeping in on a Saturday, they're out beating the bricks for their candidate. They go to caucuses on rainy or snowy nights, and they fervently believe in and support the system that most of us take for granted.

But these people are completely overshadowed by the soft-money manipulators. And sooner or later this situation breeds a deep cynicism in the very people we need to keep our politics honest and connected to mainstream America. Bad money drives out good people. That's reason enough to ban soft money.

But there's another reason as well. The fat cats aren't delivering the booty out of the goodness of their hearts. They're looking for favors in return, favors that can cost ordinary Americans real money at the very least. As former DNC fundraiser Johnny Chung put it: "The White House is like a subway—you have to put in coins to open the gates." Of course the contributions aren't limited to the presidential race. Congress is drowning in soft money. Politicians call it political support. Corporations and unions think of it as a business expense.

Soft money has helped grease the skids for several powerful industries in search of helpful legislation—helpful to them anyway. Common Cause has found plenty of signs of the old "quid pro quo" in action. I'll mention a few:

- A trade group called the Pharmaceutical Research and Manufacturers of America (PhRMA) has given more than $18.6 million in political contributions since 1991, including $8.4 million in soft-money donations. As if by magic, Congress has allowed brand-name drug companies to keep their drug patents longer. Loss of access to generic drugs costs consumers as much as $550 million a year, according to a study.

- Since 1991 the automobile, iron, and steel industries gave $5.7 million in political contributions, including more than

$1.7 million in soft money. Once again Congress responded, voting to freeze rules that would require the industry to build lighter, more fuel-efficient cars. There's no doubt that these donations paid off.

- Cable and local phone companies gave $22.8 million in political contributions since 1991, including $8.7 million in soft-money donations. While the 1996 Telecommunications Act supposedly increased competition, it led to a jump in cable and pay-phone costs of about $2.8 billion per year.

"Large soft-money contributions have obtained significant federal tax breaks and government subsidies," the group adds, "which result in a higher tax burden for the average person." Recent examples included giving television broadcasters free use of the new digital spectrum (worth up to $70 billion) and the infamous $50-billion tax break for the tobacco industry (later repealed out of embarrassment).

How did that work? The tobacco industry gave over $3 million in soft money in 1997. In return, the industry was able to get Congress to reduce the size of a proposed tax increase on tobacco by 25 percent, and also added a provision that would allow the industry to subtract the remaining tax increase from any future settlement of lawsuits underway in forty states. The source of that loophole is not in doubt. Jessica Lee, the staff director of the Joint Committee on Taxation, told *USA Today*, "The industry wrote it and submitted it . . . and we just used their language."

I'm betting most readers are completely shocked to learn that lobbyists actually write legislation. But they do. All too often, Congress acts as a rubber stamp. The *Washington Post* reported that this last-minute tobacco provision "was approved by both chambers without debate, without any acknowledgment of its sponsorship, and before many tobacco critics realized what was happening." It would probably do the same when the tobacco lobbyists and other special interests sent in directions on where to invest in the stock market. This should also further explain why I feel so strong about the stock-investment issue.

Common Cause put its finger right on the problem: "Virtually all of the Democratic Party scandals of 1996, from Roger Tamraz to John Huang, from nights in the Lincoln Bedroom to coffees with the president, stemmed from the search for soft-money contributions from corporations and wealthy donors." Our message to Congress should be clear. Take your soft money and . . . ban it.

We can scuttle soft money. It would be easy if the will—that is, grass-roots pressure—were brought to bear. The main thing we need to do is shame Congress into doing the right thing. Congress needs to know that we know what's going on and that we're sick of it. This brings to mind the old, not-very-funny joke about the three ways to change a politician's mind. In ascending order of efficiency: reason with him, shame him, shoot him. The second option is the one we should stick with.

And let's give the politicians credit. They're starting to see the light on this, no doubt because they're starting to be shamed by negative publicity. It is now safe for the most conventional, establishment pols to beat the drums against soft money. In an opinion piece in the *Washington Post*, political heavyweights Nancy Kassebaum Baker and Walter F. Mondale made the case fairly well:

A ban on soft money would not introduce any new principle into the law. It would, instead, restore a sound principle long held to be essential. That bedrock principle, developed step by step through measures signed into law by presidents from Theodore Roosevelt to Gerald Ford, is that federal election campaigns should be financed by limited contributions from individuals and not by either corporate or union treasuries. Neither candidates for federal office, nor the national political party committees whose primary mission is to elect them, should be dependent on the treasuries of corporations or unions that have strong economic interests in the decisions of the federal government.

I'm pretty much in agreement with this, except for limits on individuals. I truly believe that those limits violate the first amendment and do interfere with legitimate free speech. I'm in greater agreement with Craig Holman, project director at the National Resource Center for State and Local Campaign Finance Reform. If we ban soft money, he told the *Christian Science Monitor,* we would need to "come up with appropriately high (hard-money, individual) contribution limits to party committees, so as not to strangle them off altogether."

Why do we need to save the parties? Without them we would have a lot of freelance candidates, most of them extremely wealthy. For all their problems, parties do bring form and order to the democratic process. We don't want to destroy them. In fact we need more parties and more choices—Reform, Libertarian, maybe even Vegetarian.

My second reform would be to allow unlimited personal contributions. The cynics will be steaming over that idea, but they know in their hearts that the philosophy behind it is untouchable, because it is based on personal choice. They also know that I'm right about putting the individual at the heart of the process—not the politicians, not the corporate CEO, not the union boss, but the individual American.

But they are convinced that if individuals were allowed to give as much to campaigns as they desired, guys like me would take over politics. They believe in personal freedom all right, so long as guys like Trump are kept in harness.

I believe that if you want to give your life's savings to Al Gore, that should be between you, Al Gore, and your psychiatrist. I also believe that if I am dumb enough to think I can buy a high office for one of my pals, I should be allowed to do so. Believe me, the networks would love me for it. Think of all the ad money.

Of course, if I think I can buy a national office for somebody, I definitely need to see that psychiatrist myself. Let's be sensible. If a huge expenditure of personal funds were a guarantee of political victory, our current president would be either Steve Forbes or Ross Perot.

Will Americans go for this idea of unlimited personal support? I believe they will, because Americans, unlike a lot of politicians and policy wonks, truly do believe in personal freedom. They take it as a given that a person should have the right to support a candidate as passionately as they choose.

The vast majority of Americans considers giving money to a politician to be an un-American activity. They are deeply skeptical of those in high office, and usually for good reason. When Americans look to those at the top of the political game, especially in the past couple of years, their eyes roll. Whether it's Bill Clinton discussing what the definition of "is" is, or Newt Gingrich pouting because he had to exit a plane through the back door, there's plenty to laugh at. Jay Leno will never run short of material.

There's something else to keep in mind as well. The limit on personal giving obscures the way political fundraising really works. Let me explain this from a personal perspective. I am more than happy to use my influence to back people who I think mean well for our country. I do it all the time. In fact I get very enthusiastic about some candidates and go out of my way to help them. My reason is very simple. I've seen what incompetent politicians can do to a community. They almost ruined the city I live in.

And let me assure you that limits on personal giving mean absolutely nothing. As already mentioned, personal contributions to a candidate are limited to $1,000 (and $20,000 per year to a party). This was passed as a reform measure after the Nixon upheavals, the belief being that this would keep the fat cats at bay. Of course it did nothing of the sort. A fat cat will always find a way to get money to his or her candidate.

The untold fact is that this limit on personal gifts has made it even easier for people with money to ingratiate themselves with politicians. They can simply strike a check to anyone who asks. The limit makes no difference. What makes a difference to campaigns is the fundraising events. I've hosted fundraisers for a number of candidates and have easily raised several million dollars in an evening. There's no law against that, and there shouldn't be. If anyone thinks that limiting personal donations to $1,000 in any way cleans up the process, they're just not familiar with how the system works.

But I do believe that this limit undermines our basic freedom of expression. Free speech is, alongside freedom of conscience, at the very foundation of our society. And when you say a person can only speak to the tune of $1,000 you may be severely limiting his vocabulary.

So why do we put up with laws that restrict a person's right to fully support a candidacy that reflects their deepest belief in how this nation should be run? We allow pornographers free rein, but keep hard-working, idealistic, and politically engaged citizens on a short leash.

To sum up, we should ban soft money and allow individuals to fully exercise their political consciences. Those are two great reforms.

The third leg of the Trump political reform is also simple and vital. I believe that Americans should know immediately who is giving what to whom. If we have full participation, we should also have full and fast disclosure.

I really do believe that most Americans are in favor of individuals being allowed to support candidates to whatever degree they choose. They might also believe that special interests should be allowed to make contributions at some levels. I believe they would set relatively high levels if they could be assured of knowing who is spending the big money on political campaigns. My goal is to make sure this information is readily available.

In fact I fully believe that if we shifted our focus to the donor side of politics instead of basing our voting decisions on speeches, press releases, and "debates," we would have a much better informed public. You can learn a lot more about a politician from knowing who put the money in his pocket than you can learn from what he or she might happen to chirp from a podium.

Who does he work for?

If your candidate is taking a lot of money from a tobacco baron, for example, you should have a pretty good idea where he or she is going to stand on liability issues. If a lot of money is coming in from a person who is a well-known figure in a teachers' union, and you happen to support school choice—I mean real school choice—you'd better find another candidate to support. Follow the money, the old Watergate line goes. If we know where a candidate's backing comes from, we can make the most informed of all possible choices.

I also don't think we should allow contributions from non-U.S. citizens. Like everyone else, I was amazed at the stories about how certain Chinese gardeners (and Buddhist nuns) were making big-dollar contributions to the Clinton campaign. But the fact is that allowing non-citizens to influence national elections is a scandal. Both parties look overseas for money, and this should be banned. I honestly believe that the Clinton administration's foreign policy was deeply affected by their illegal overseas donors.

FULL DISCLOSURE

My plan is not complicated. First we should pass legislation that would require campaigns to electronically post donors and donations at the close of each business day.

This is a perfect wedding of the information and reform revolutions. When a candidate accepts a donation from executives at Philip Morris or Planned Parenthood, we would know about it that same day. Constant disclosure would also assure steady press scrutiny instead of the clumps of coverage of the sporadic reports that campaigns currently submit, which are so easy to ignore.

In fact constant disclosure would make a tremendously interesting story, much more so than the constant drip, drip, drip of platitudes and petty scandals that comprise traditional campaign coverage. If I were running a cable network, for example, I would gladly run speeches by serious candidates (and by fringe candidates as well, just to keep things spicy). What I would add, however, would be a running line at the bottom of the screen listing the day's, or perhaps the week's, donations—like the stock ticker than runs at the bottom of financial network telecasts.

The public value would be immense, not to mention humorous. Imagine, for example, Al Gore delivering a wimpy speech on movie violence as the ticker pointed out the big lump of Hollywood gold that had dropped in his pocket that afternoon. This reform alone could force candidates to exercise more scrutiny in the people they take on as supporters. It would also make for some very good television.

One more reform that I know Americans will support, almost without exception, has to do with the clearly troubling phenomenon of having public officials begging for donations from the very people they are supposed to be regulating—while they are regulating them.

Americans support a wall of separation between church and state because it protects their religious organizations from government encroachment, and also because it ensures that no denomination or faith is able to seize power.

Similarly we need to erect a tall wall of separation between policymakers and the people they are supposed to be regulating. We can't erect an absolute wall, of course. There are free association issues involved. But we could pass legislation that would simply state that if you're making policy you cannot simultaneously solicit money. This should be true for Congress, the president, and any member of the executive branch.

I've made it very clear that I don't think private citizens are corrupting politics by contributing to like-minded candidates. But there is no doubt whatsoever that when a cabinet member solicits funds it sends the message that their policy decisions are for sale.

The same is true for congressmen, who should not be allowed to solicit or accept any funds while the people's business is being done. When Congress is not in session, members can beg to their hearts' content—remembering, of course, that the proceeds will be posted at day's end. The fact that this isn't the law is, to my mind, a huge scandal. But it won't be changed until the people demand it.

★   ★   ★

Looking for the absolutely foolproof test to determine who's a regular politician and who isn't? This is it. Politicians are on the take and looking for job security. Not me.

Nothing I have mentioned in this chapter is expensive. There is nothing here that cannot be done quickly, and the benefits would be enormous. Banning soft money, restricting fundraising by officials, and reporting on campaign financing in real time would bring about real changes, and bring them quickly.

I believe the time is right for reform. The people are ready, willing, and fed up with the status quo. We're seeing the passion for reform in the new breed of politicians—and nonpoliticians—we are electing. Americans haven't given up on their system, but they have looked at the x-rays and they see some troubling shadows. It's time to open up the patient and start cutting. The pols may scream a little, but as the old saying goes, no pain no gain.

CHAPTER TEN

Volunteering:
The American Way

I'M GOING TO SPEAK DIFFERENTLY in this chapter than I have in the others about recreating the American Dream. So far I've uncovered plenty to find fault with—overregulation of businesses and individuals, excessive taxation, misguided leniency in schools and courthouses, willful ignorance about dangers we face right now and dangers we will meet in the future.

But however critical I've been, I don't mean that all the people who have run this country badly for decades are bad people. Some have been, but many were not. Many reformers and social planners mean well. They want the best for their fellow citizens and for mankind in general. Many are like those who, in their hopes of rehabilitating criminals, endanger whole neighborhoods; they want the best but don't know the right way to get it.

Often plans and programs that are transparently stupid come from the sponsors' deep ignorance of human nature and the laws of economics. Has Trump turned philosopher? No. But I think—to paraphrase Jack Maple, the great city transit cop who worked with Commissioner Bratton and Mayor Giuliani to rid New York of crime—that anybody who thinks seriously about their work *is* a philosopher. I think that being in business has taught me how to motivate people and how to make organizations work efficiently. Many politicians who have spent their lives locked up inside the system have gotten out of touch. They don't know what's going on in America.

The great failed social programs of our country were trying to create a sense of community in which the elderly, the poor, and the disadvantaged were taken care of. What many reformers failed to see was that there is, already in place in America, an informal, decentralized, unregulated group of volunteers who are now and have for a long time been in the business of delivering on the American Dream. If we want the dream to stay alive we should permit these volunteers to continue their work unobstructed. We should nurture the individuals and groups who are holding our neighborhoods and cities together.

Around the world Americans have a reputation for brashness and selfishness and worship of the dollar. The image isn't entirely wrong. America does love success. I know I do. This is without a doubt the most achiever-friendly nation on earth. We worship people who do well—even those who may be disasters as human beings. Think of all the sports figures whose off-field antics are negative but who are still adored. America also admires high achievers from business, the arts, science, education, and even politics. We don't have kings and queens. Instead our royalty is made up of people who work hard, play hard, and make their way to the top. We treat our achievers like Greek gods. I know this phenomenon all too well. I'm a real estate guy—a successful one—and as a result of my success I've got people following my every move.

Yet there's a funny twist to this tale. Americans also love their saints—people who reach out to help those who aren't making it on their own, for whatever reason—including self-inflicted defeat. I'm not talking only about obvious saints such as the late Mother Teresa, whom I once crossed paths with. When she was trying to build a New York facility to care for hurting people, she ran into ridiculous regulations. I know the good Mother reacted in a holier fashion than I tend to when confronted with bureaucratic nonsense, but it is interesting to note that the New York City government, at least pre-Giuliani, made life tough even for an undisputed saint.

Americans admired Mother Teresa and they also admire their everyday saints—those people who quietly lend a hand to down-and-out Bowery bums, reach out to tough kids from tough homes, and work with prisoners and junkies as well as teens who need help getting their foot on the first rung of the ladder. Give yourself a little quiz: Who is more admired in your community—the president of a local firm that may employ thousands of people, or the man or woman who runs a charitable foundation on a shoestring? All of us should be and usually are hugely thankful for the job-creators, because without them we have no work, no prosperity, and no means by which to help others. But our admiration is unmatched for the volunteer who visits the AIDS patient in the hospital, tries to get the Bowery hardtimer a job, or who teaches an inner-city kid not only that he can read but also that his or her life has meaning and promise. Achievers are royalty in this country, but royalty will always play second fiddle to saints.

The failure of many of our political and social programs comes from our failure to recognize the saints in our midst; from our failure to see the very holy work being done by the generous, responsible people all around us.

The great thing, of course, is that you can be both successful and generous. Not only could be, but should be. All of us have an obligation to use our talents not only to pursue our individual dreams but also to help others achieve their dreams, no matter how humble they might be.

That's the belief that is behind this chapter. I'm going to give an endorsement to the great American tradition of volunteering, whether by lending personal talents or by contributing to charitable causes. You are not a full citizen of this great country unless you give back to society in a way that's *not* required.

Don't get me wrong. I'm not overlooking the immense social value derived from paying taxes and creating jobs. Almost all of us take for granted the entrepreneurs and businesspeople who create the financial stability that holds this country together. We have totally lost sight of the fact that taxpayers—almost all of us over the age of twenty-one—are the unsung heroes of our society. Few of us take the time to recognize that the towns, cities, states, and country we live in are testaments to personal productivity. When we do our jobs we're not only helping ourselves, we're also helping our communities.

However, I want to talk about going above and beyond the duties of citizenship. I want to talk about the things we do to help others because helping is simply the right thing to do. I like the line Oklahoma congressman J. C. Watts uses to define the truly good person: He or she is the one who does good even when nobody is looking.

While it's the rare politician who steps foot in a homeless shelter without first alerting the press, the volunteers I'm talking about are not glory-seekers. The volunteer I admire is the person who helps others even though nobody notices the quiet good citizens—and America is full of them.

When it comes to public service, in my family we never particularly advertised. My sister Maryanne says she can't picture me as a gray lady handing out bandages, and it's true. I think there are more effective ways to use my time to personally attend to others. My father had only one of his charities attached to his name, the Trump Pavilion for Nursing and Rehabilitation at Jamaica Hospital. He also contributed to Temple Share Zion synagogue in Brooklyn and the Creedmore Hospital in Queens. Many of his other charities are less well known. I know that many of his acts of charity—acts of kindness and courage and generosity shown to friends and relatives of friends—were unrecorded.

VOLUNTEERS

Millions upon millions of people fall into the category of true volunteer. In fact the United States is unparalleled in volunteering and charitable giving. Let's look at the numbers—numbers that truly amazed me as I pulled them together. I knew this was a generous country, but I had no idea Americans were this generous.

Nearly half—48.8 percent—of the adult population does volunteer work of some type. All told, about a hundred million Americans pitch in.

Consider this: The highest percentage of household income to charities comes from households that make under $10,000 a year. Bill Gates's magnificent gift of one billion dollars to fund a twenty-year program to finance scholarships for minority students is truly commendable. But the gift represented a little over 1 percent of Gates's net worth. Ted Turner's gift of Time Warner stock worth $100 million for the work of the UN was also admirable. But because of the way the gift was structured, it may actually cost him nothing. There are many poor people in this country who tithe to their parish church. That means—no smoke and mirrors—they really give up 10 percent of what they make.

Here are a few more facts and figures on charitable giving from a group called Independent Sector: The number of institutions and organizations established to serve community purposes totals over 740,000. When you add in religious congregations, which often provide extensive community services, that number rises above a million. And when community groups and local chapters of larger groups are included, the number rises close to two million.

This incredible level of volunteer activity tells us a great deal about America's heart, and we should not let the cynics get away with obscuring this part of our national character.

The most amazing thing about all this is that the numbers could be even higher. People at middle income level contribute a lower percentage to charity than either the rich or the very poor. The reason is that the middle class is paying most of the bills in this country; if you let this sector keep more of its money, it will distribute more to people in need.

HIGHER TAXES, LESS CHARITY

Let people keep more of their money and they'll spread it around in their communities—much more efficiently than the government could ever hope to.

High taxes restrict a citizen's ability to support the causes and charities that speak to his or her heart. As I've already pointed out, many people volunteer and contribute from a sense of religious principle. Many would like to give more but can't because of their tax burden. This is especially true of the middle class, which government perpetually ransacks. I am amazed, in fact, at the level to which the middle class does contribute and volunteer.

There is no doubt that when high levies stand in the way of serving the less fortunate, the lives of contributors are diminished in a moral and spiritual sense. They feel they should do more but cannot. Potential recipients, of course, suffer as well. If that's not immorality, then what is it?

There's no denying that lower taxes tend to translate into increased charitable giving. Clearly, if people really wanted lower taxes simply because they were greedy, residents of low-tax states would be less likely to give to charity. Instead, the money not going toward taxes would be spent on cars, bass boats, and vacations.

But the facts are completely the opposite. People in low-tax states—people who get to keep more of their own money—are, as a whole, more generous than their counterparts in high-tax states.

A study by the National Conference of State Legislatures, for example, found that the most generous Americans tend to reside in the most lightly taxed states.

There's a mistaken image of the volunteer. We still tend to think of the hospital candy striper, often a suburban housewife who takes time from her busy life to pitch in, or the church ladies and gentlemen who run the inner-city reading programs. These types of people are incredibly valuable and there are many of them. But they don't tell the whole story.

Consider how an increasing number of Americans celebrate Martin Luther King Jr. Day—not merely with a barbecue or an afternoon nap, but doing volunteer work. This year ten thousand people in Philadelphia volunteered to clean up schools, streets, and neighborhoods. That's up from one thousand in 1994.

There has been a dramatic rise in what are called City Cares organizations, which connect volunteers with projects that need their help. At the end of the 1980s there were two such organizations, one in New York and one in Washington, D.C. Now there are twenty-seven of them coordinating work for a hundred thousand volunteers.

Look to the top of American society and you'll find volunteers. Lots of them. The best and brightest work alongside the ordinary citizen. Colin Powell, former head of the Joint Chiefs of Staff, is heading up a volunteer effort called America's Promise, dedicated to helping millions of kids, especially inner-city children, to reach their potential. Former Presidents Carter and Bush have also been part of this effort. These guys don't have to do this. They have been to the very top and still influence policy decisions, write books, and live well. But they know what I've already said: If you don't give back, you're not fully a citizen of this country.

General Powell's group is pushing an agenda based on five principles: Mentoring, Protecting, Nurturing, Preparing, and Serving. Its volunteers want to prepare these kids to take their place in the working world, and they also want to teach them that their duty is to serve others. Powell set a goal of recruiting two million volunteers to his effort and has already received large commitments from industry. Timberland Inc. said it would donate five thousand pairs of boots to inner-city kids, while Columbia/HCA Healthcare Corp. pledged to immunize one million kids by the year 2000. The list goes on and on.

A group called Volunteers in Medicine provides free care to people who do not have medical insurance. Another group of twelve thousand retired executives gives advice and counsel to three hundred thousand small businesses through a program called Service Corps of Retired Executives. These retirees are not only helping others, but themselves as well. Those who participate are less depressed, more satisfied, and feel in better control of their lives.

We're seeing an unprecedented effort by business to encourage employees to volunteer. A survey of businesses by the Points of Light Foundation and the Conference Board found that 92 percent of executives say they encourage their employees to volunteer.

There's no doubt that some executives have concluded that volunteering is good for the bottom line, and so they encourage it. I say, so what? If volunteering helps a company while helping the less fortunate, that's a win-win situation. Are we supposed to be against win-win situations?

In fact the way in which charity and capitalism serve each other underscores the beauty of our system. People who hate business—a contingent of professors and entertainers, and some millionaires in the media—want us to believe that making a living in our system is only about greed. We're all in it for ourselves, and damn the other guy. Ebenezer Scrooge is on their wanted poster, and if you want a more current illustration of this mind-set in action check out prime-time television and the movies. The presentation of businessmen is almost always negative. We're the bad guys, just waiting for an opportunity to shut down an orphanage or foreclose on their grandmothers, preferably both on the same day.

The truth, of course, is almost entirely the opposite. Capitalism is based on markets, and if you're going to make it in the marketplace you're going to have to serve people. George Gilder, an advocate of supply-side economics and author of *Wealth and Poverty*, has pointed out that capitalism is mainly about pleasing others. Please or perish. We serve each other in order to survive and prosper. Sure there's self-interest involved. But again, so what? Those who decry self-interest insist that self-interest is a bad thing. But the opposite is true. Self-interest has produced the most generous society on earth—ours.

Capitalism works because it is based on a true reading of human nature, one that recognizes not only self-interest but also the benefit of helping others. Volunteerism is much the same. It benefits the recipients and the donors as well.

HELPING AT ALL LEVELS

I'm going to briefly look at some other volunteer efforts around the country. There are so many that I can only skim over a few. But first I want to talk about some of the volunteer activities I've supported through the years. This is not to make myself look good. As anybody who knows me will tell you, I've never been one who tried to pass himself off as a saint.

Instead, my purpose in going into my own work is twofold: One, to show how we can take the same skills that help us professionally and use them to help our communities. And two, that no matter what your standing and no matter your accomplishments, lending a hand to someone else brings the same personal rewards and a sense of community that can be achieved in no other way.

Let's take my first point. I'm a billionaire. I came by my wealth not by magic but by organizing and utilizing my time and talents. I'm good at making deals and at seeing projects through. I know how to organize. I know how to motivate. And I know how to get right in the middle of a project and push it across the finish line. The money is the afterthought; my thrill comes from making the project work. I am hugely fortunate that I am financially rewarded while I use my skills doing something I enjoy.

The larger lesson is that whatever your talents happen to be, you can put them to use as a volunteer. I wrote earlier about my work on the Wollman Skating Rink in Central Park. The city's efforts were dismal and disastrous. It was like a kindergarten class trying to build a jet fighter. When I took over, the transformation was instantaneous.

Why? This was just another piece of work for the city. Nothing special—just an ice-skating rink. The project caught my attention because I saw in it a way of putting my skills to work for my community. I knew I could make something good for my fellow citizens, and I liked the idea of doing everything to finish the job quickly and efficiently. While I believe I will be remembered for bigger projects than a skating rink, few things I've done have brought me more pleasure than doing this project for my fellow New Yorkers, and for those who visit our city.

Another project I got involved in was Harlem Hospital, which was having a terrible time with its elevators. How terrible? For one thing, even some of the people who worked on the top floors of the eighteen-story building would use the stairs because at least they were dependable. Of course bad elevators also impeded the work of doctors and made it hard to transport patients. This was totally unacceptable. When I heard about it, a little light went on. After all, I know something about elevators. I also have a couple of buildings that are a bit higher than eighteen stories. Because I was uniquely positioned to lend a hand in this case, I lent my services and those of my elevator repair people to Harlem Hospital.

Another case that was a perfect fit was Andrew Ten, who lived in California. He needed desperately to come to the East Coast because a very rare and very dangerous medical condition threatened his life. His parents felt that they had exhausted the medical options in the West and wanted this brave three-year-old to have the best shot possible at overcoming his challenge. They wanted him to be seen by doctors at the Long Island Jewish Medical Center.

The problem was that the commercial airlines refused to fly the child. He couldn't leave his home without a portable oxygen tank, a suction machine, a device to help him breathe, and other medical gear. Like all good parents, Andrew's searched high and low for a solution. Eventually they called me. Though I had never heard of this family, my heart immediately went out to them. And when it was time, so did my Boeing 737, with three nurses on board. Again, I was qualified to lend a hand. People told me that I didn't have to do that for this family. But that misses the point. If you are in a position to help, you help.

Not all charitable acts are life-and-death situations and, in fact, I've found that it's nice to support a diversity of causes. If you get involved in a variety of causes you're going to find out more about America, and that is going to give you a deeper appreciation for our country and the people who have made it what it is.

One day New York Councilman Enoch Williams asked if I would be interested in taking a trip over to the Crown Heights section of Brooklyn. He wanted me to see a place called Weeksville, which is one of the earliest Black settlements in New York. The settlement is believed to have been founded by James Weeks, a free Black American, sometime around 1838. Researchers discovered four small frame houses in 1969 that were part of the settlement.

Unfortunately, the houses were in very bad shape and there were few funds to keep this vital piece of New York's history from crumbling into dust.

I was immediately convinced that Weeksville must be saved. I feel very fortunate to have been able to protect this site. It is extremely important for all of us to know about our history, including how brave African Americans overcame immense obstacles in the pursuit of their American dream. If Councilman Williams hadn't invited me to join this campaign, I probably would not have ever known this interesting and inspiring story.

Here's one more story from my personal scrapbook. I've told it before, but it hits so close to protecting the American Dream that I think it's worth telling again.

I saw a story on the news about Annabel Hill, who'd hit bottom. Her sixty-seven-year-old husband had committed suicide—believing his insurance would help his wife keep their Georgia farm, which had been in the family for generations. But it still wasn't enough money and she was facing foreclosure.

So I got in touch with a man named Frank Argenbright who was trying to help her out, and he put me in touch with the bank that held Annabel's mortgage. A vice president there told me that he was sorry but there was nothing he could do; the auctioning of the farm was scheduled to proceed.

That was just too much. Here was a family that had worked hard to keep their dream alive, only to see it snatched away in the most merciless way. So I told the banker that a different fate awaited Annabel Hill, and that if he didn't back off I was going to personally bring a lawsuit against the bank. The charge would be harassing Mr. Hill to death. The banker swallowed half the air in Georgia and hung up. Then he called back and assured me something could be worked out.

That's when I decided to get involved. By this time the media had heard about the phone call and it became a lead story. People began to send in contributions. Don Imus, the broadcaster whose crusty growl can't hide his golden heart, was very involved in the effort and his listeners contributed significantly. It wasn't long before we were hosting a mortgage-burning party in the lobby of my little spread on Fifth Avenue.

Financially this was obviously no big deal. But in human terms, there aren't words to express what Annabel Hill gave to me. Most of us have a few things in life we would never give back, no matter what. Helping Annabel is that way for me.

I'm sure about one thing: The deepest part of our nature goes unfulfilled if we ignore people who are in need.

As I've pointed out, about a hundred million of us do some kind of volunteer work. There's plenty to do. As former President George Bush said in a major speech on volunteering, there's a great deal that needs to be done, especially with kids:

> Every thirteen seconds a child somewhere in America is abused. Every thirty seconds a child is born into poverty. Every fifty-nine seconds a child is born to a teen mother. Every five minutes a child is arrested for violent crime and every two hours a child is killed by gunfire. It is an understatement to say that these statistics don't paint a pretty picture for the future.

George Bush is absolutely right. Kids are the future of this country. My heart especially goes out to people who work with kids, and I'm always on the lookout for a group that is doing the hard and often thankless job of helping kids who have been dealt a lousy hand in life.

What could be tougher, for example, than to be the child of a prison inmate? As mentioned in an earlier chapter, most inmates are males, so it's likely to be the father who's in jail. He then can't support the family either emotionally or economically. The family is probably living in poverty, or very close to the edge. The child is feeling like a social outcast, and definitely thinking that no one could care less about his or her life.

Then, close to Christmas, there's a knock at the door. It's someone from the Angel Tree program, a part of Prison Fellowship. This is a group founded by ex–Watergate felon Charles Colson. Talk about a turnaround. Colson went to jail, and now spends most of his time working with prisoners. At Christmas the Angel Tree people distribute presents to the children of prisoners. Their goals are humble: one toy and one piece of clothing. They're also telling these kids that some stranger out there cares for them. That's a connection that's more valuable than the presents.

Or consider an organization called the Orphan Foundation of America. Here's a group that reflects everything good about volunteering, from its origins to its mission to its strict reliance on private funding to the successes it can claim—successes that come against all odds. I want to start from the beginning because this organization has a very interesting, and very American, history.

Joseph Rivers (whose moving story was told by James G. Zumwalt in *Parade* magazine) was in the foster-care system most of his life. That is tough in and of itself. It's bad enough when a kid is removed from his home, even if home life may be hellish, but what happens next can be torture: Siblings are separated, kids often bounce from one home to another, and then when they turn eighteen their support checks stop and they suddenly face the world on their own. That's what happened to Joseph Rivers. He "aged out" at eighteen with no place to go and no one to really help him get his start in the world.

He could have cast himself as a victim, but instead Joseph Rivers made himself into an American hero. Quietly he struggled for seventeen years, never losing sight of who he was and the idea that he had something unique to offer kids who had come up as he did. In 1981 he decided to establish the Orphan Foundation. His mission was simple, and no different than what most parents try to do for their own children: He wanted to spare others the hardships he had endured.

By now ordained in the Liberal Catholic Church, Father Rivers began building his dream, working in donated space in a church basement, raising support and volunteers wherever he could. But, sadly, he died before the organization really came into its own.

It would have been easy for his few surviving supporters to throw in the towel. After all, there weren't many of them to begin with. There was very little money. But there remained a need. There remained the spirit of Joseph Rivers. And there was also a volunteer named Eileen McCaffrey.

Eileen's mother had been a foster parent, taking in a stream of orphans. One of them had moved on when Eileen was four years old, but he had made a deep impact on her, and as she grew up she often wondered what had become of him. That orphan was none other than Joseph Rivers. Eileen had finally caught up with him, only to see her long lost "brother" die too soon.

So McCaffrey and her small group stuck with it. She is now the executive director of the Orphan Foundation, which is located in suburban Washington, D.C. It has two full-time employees, including McCaffrey, and about sixty volunteers. Until I became interested in this group, I hadn't realized this particular area of need: There are around a half million American kids in foster care.

Because of the instability in their lives, less than 50 percent of these kids graduate from high school. And one study acknowledged by the foundation discovered that up to 40 percent of these kids will join the ranks of the homeless sometime in their lives.

Enter the Orphan Foundation. Besides mentoring kids and helping them along during their foster-care years, it is also trying to put as many of them as possible into college. Their college-bound program is called the Oliver Project, named after that irrepressible Dickens character, Oliver Twist (who would no doubt do very well in business should he suddenly spring to life). So far, these people have provided nearly $700,000 in scholarships to kids in forty-four states— without taking one cent of public money. And they have worked wonders with some very tough cases.

Take a kid named Anthony Peebles from Akron, as reported by Donna Robb in the Cleveland *Plain Dealer.* He never knew his father. After giving birth to him in 1978, his mother had seven more kids. She was a prostitute. She couldn't take care of him and left him with a grandmother who in turn left him with an aunt and her boyfriend, both drug dealers.

"I saw the easy money every night," he once told a reporter. "I don't know why I didn't go that way. My brothers and sisters adapted to that life. I was the outcast."

But he also had his version of the American Dream. Anthony was his high school class treasurer, worked on the yearbook, and joined the Future Educators of America when he was a freshman. He tutored students at St. Matthew's parish, joined a local theater group, attended a Pentecostal church, and got a job in a restaurant. He finally graduated from school with a 3.2 grade point average and got a Foundation scholarship to the University of Akron.

He could have easily succumbed to the philosophy that says he's a victim. There is plenty of encouragement along those lines. Instead he saw that America offers opportunity for those who will reach out for it. He grabbed for the brass ring, and I think he already has a piece of it.

Eileen McCaffrey makes a point that we tend to forget in this the age of vast welfare programs:

We have an obligation to provide food and shelter, but that's not enough. These kids need to know that somebody cares for them, that somebody has singled them out and wants to help them along. That is absolutely necessary for teaching kids values. Larger programs can reinforce values, but you have to have that personal contact to really teach kids about right and wrong. Without personal involvement, they just don't have a sense that anyone cares for them.

This group has sent kids to the best schools, including MIT, and has also put them in touch with the country's leadership, both political and in the media. That's important so that these kids know they are not social outcasts, and it's also good for the people at the top. It reminds them that they are needed.

Eileen McCaffrey shows us that caring is contagious. Here's a basically one-woman shop on a mission to help orphans. She gets a scholarship program going that helps kids in most every state in the Union. She holds events in Washington that are underwritten by giants like Gateway 2000, American Airlines, Cellular One, and General Electric. She wants kids to meet their political leaders, and suddenly they're in the offices of Representatives J. C. Watts, James Talent, James Walsh, Mike Neumann, Lynn Woolsey, Maurice Hinchey, Joe Kennedy, Tom Sawyer, Steve Largent, William Coyne, and William Clinger. They were also welcomed by Senators John Ashcroft, Ernest Hollings, Barbara Boxer, John Warner, Charles Robb, Arlen Specter, and Rick Santorum.

These kids came out of the most troubled homes and had miserable prospects, but when one adult and a few volunteers decided to touch their lives, big doors opened. Don't think this doesn't make a big impression on these kids. It teaches them that they are valued members of society, no matter what their background. Or, as Ronald Reagan would say, it shows them that America is a place of destinations, not origins.

★   ★   ★

I could write a very large book on volunteers. But I could only skim the surface for this chapter. From the abolitionist cause against slavery to the civil rights crusade; from medical and educational work in the inner cities to the Appalachian hollows, volunteers have done most of the heavy lifting.

We should back public policies that encourage, not discourage, this purest form of public service—particularly tax reduction, which would leave more money in the hands of the middle class. And while the need can be overwhelming, I think there's a good rule we can follow: Find one person to help. Sure, some of us help a lot more than one person. But find one kid who can't read, or one single mother who's having a hard time raising her kids, and help them. It will open a new world for both of you.

We should never let the cynics obscure the volunteer spirit of the American character. Americans can be wild, loud, pushy, tough-minded, and even rude, crude, hot, and nasty. But America is also a land of saints. It is our honor to live among them.

CHAPTER ELEVEN

Should I Run?

L AST MAY A WASHINGTON-BASED Democratic pollster,
Rob Schroth, conducted a nationwide survey of one thousand
voters. Schroth's thesis was that figures from disciplines outside
of politics were better known and more trusted than the current crop
of politicians seeking the U.S. presidency. Schroth tested athletes,
businessmen, newscasters, and entertainers; he tested the popularity
of public figures like Clint Eastwood, Michael Jordan, Barbra
Streisand, Bill Gates, Katie Couric, Ted Turner, Robert Redford,
Barbara Walters, John Elway, and Donald Trump.

It was no surprise to me that 97 percent of the American people
knew who I was. It was also no surprise that I was particularly popular with some segments of the American population. Working
people, African Americans, Latinos, and people making under
$25,000 a year all had a favorable opinion. Rich people did not like
me. Rich people who don't know me *never* like me. Rich people who
know me like me.

Let's face it, if I run it will be a boon to the political cartoonists and late-night talk-show hosts. But I can take it. My experience in the New York real estate world has given me a pretty thick skin; even I laugh at the editorial cartoons that show Trump with money bulging out of his pockets.

What was astounding about the poll though was the fact that when tested in a whimsical three-way race with Texas Governor George W. Bush and Vice President Al Gore, Bush led narrowly with 35 percent, Trump was second with 31 percent, and Al Gore was third with 30 percent. I was amused but thought no more about it. A few weeks later the *National Enquirer* published a poll of their readers that showed an identical result: Bush narrowly leading Trump with Gore bringing up the rear. I know that the Washington elite will snicker about the *National Enquirer*, but I recall the late Republican National Chairman Lee Atwater, one of the most successful political strategists of the '80s, once saying that he read the *Enquirer* regularly to keep his finger on the pulse of the average American.

Sometimes the Washington big shots forget that not everyone went to Yale or Harvard, that not everyone is making six figures a year, and that the average Americans are the people to whom the politicians in this country are accountable.

As I mentioned in the introduction, this is not the first time I've been encouraged to run for office. After New York City had spent $20 million and seven years trying to fix the Wollman Skating Rink in Central Park, I stepped in and did the job in three months for $2.25 million. People urged me to run for mayor because they saw I could get things done. A few years later, New York Republicans urged me to run against Governor Mario Cuomo. Both times I appreciated the faith shown in my abilities, but I declined. I was busy making things happen my own way.

This time, however, there was clearly some very serious interest in me, so I took advantage of it. In May the *Wall Street Journal* published an article of mine on Bill Bradley and the disastrous Tax Relief Act of 1986. In June the *Miami Herald* published a second article I wrote, this time on Castro's miserable record on human rights.

Last summer I was contacted by two gentlemen who said they met on the Internet in a chatroom. Tim Whitcomb, a young independent film producer in Los Angeles, and Ira Cohen, a sixty-three-year-old vegetable broker in New Jersey, had formed the Draft Trump in 2000 Committee. I was flattered, but I told a *New York Times* reporter that I loved what I'm doing now and that I wasn't interested.

The following weekend I was watching CNN Headline News and there was an item regarding the Reform Party national convention being held in Dearborn, Michigan.

I was stunned to see footage of delegates carrying enormous Trump banners, but even more surprised by a poll conducted by EPIC-MRA, a nonpartisan Lansing, Michigan–based survey research firm of convention delegates and participants. The straw poll showed Ross Perot as the number-one preference for the party's 2000 presidential nomination, but showed Trump as a surprisingly strong second choice with 20.6 percent of the vote. Interestingly, Pat Buchanan received only 7.8 percent of the vote. Clearly, Whitcomb and Cohen had not abandoned their cause. There was enough of a buzz at the convention that I had to issue a statement thanking people for their interest in me.

The

THE AMERICA WE DESERVE

A few days later I spoke by phone with Jesse Ventura. He told me he was keeping his powder dry, but mildly encouraged me to make the race. I told him I'd think about it.

I began to consider running for president the same way I consider any major business decision: I assemble all the information, ask all the right questions, think through all the possible scenarios, and most important of all, go to the best authorities for advice. After that, I rely on my instincts.

In considering a presidential run, I turned to a friend of long standing who has represented me for eighteen years in Washington, D.C. Roger Stone is a veteran of eight national presidential campaigns and is largely credited with the public rehabilitation of President Richard Nixon, from his resignation in 1974 until his death. I met Roger in 1979 when he was organizing the northeastern United States for Ronald Reagan's presidential campaign. We were introduced by Roy Cohn, the flamboyant attorney who sometimes represented me. Cohn told me Stone was the single toughest guy he knew. That was quite a comment coming from Roy, who was no pussycat.

I asked Stone to assess what a bid for the Reform Party presidential nomination would cost and to figure out the logistics, timing, and mechanism necessary to win. I'm convinced that I can decide whether to run in early 2000 and still have time to take all comers for the Reform Party nod. The party will choose its nominee in August of 2000.

By September, though major opinion-makers in the media were generally skeptical about my candidacy, they began to take more and more notice. When *New York Times* columnist Maureen Dowd called

264

me, a lot of my friends urged me not to return the call. Maureen has a reputation for having skewered some pretty big guys in her journalistic career. President Bush was said to particularly despise her, due to her barbed and lethal criticism. Richard Nixon once told me admiringly that "she has the sharpest pen in the business." I gave Maureen the interview she wanted and found her to be incredibly smart, insightful, honest, and fair.

By the end of summer, Dowd's was one of many newspaper columns discussing the possibility that I might run for president.

I was in Las Vegas golfing with my friend Sammy Lee, the representative of Henry Chang, one of the richest guys in Hong Kong, when my office in New York contacted me to tell me that I had an urgent message to call Governor Ventura. We played phone tag throughout the weekend, but when we finally spoke Jesse encouraged me again—this time more vehemently—to seek the Reform Party nomination. He told me he intended to go public with his view that Trump would be a strong and viable nominee for the Reform Party and that, in his opinion, I could win.

He told a Washington paper, *The Hill:*

I'm getting very intrigued by Donald Trump. . . . He's like me. He offers a very successful businessman who knows how to do business. He [is] an out-of-the-box character like me who can paint these other two candidates with the same brush I did. I think he's a dynamic speaker. . . . I think he could be very serious . . . . I think be brings a lot to the table for us in the Reform Party—not only could he get that money that we already have coming, but he doesn't need a whole lot

of fundraising if he so desires. And right now, what's important to us in the Reform Party is to have a viable candidate
who's different from the other two [major parties]. And I like
the idea of another non-career politician. . . . He's kind of
leading the charge . . . right now.

Ventura was not interested in Buchanan. He said, "I don't want a
retread from another party."

Even though I promised Jesse I would consider a campaign
more seriously, I still was not convinced that it was the best thing
for me.

But by now there were many articles in national newspapers and
magazines such as *USA Today, Time,* and *Newsweek.* I was asked to make
appearances on *Dateline NBC, Today, Larry King Live, Good Morning
America, Meet the Press, Face the Nation,* and *This Week.*

Moreover, it seemed that issues that concern me were receiving
public attention. *Nightline,* for example, did a five-part series in early
October on bioterrorism. Then, to my surprise, Pat Buchanan
announced that he would bolt the Republican Party and seek the
Reform Party nomination. A year before the election Buchanan already
looks to me like a loser. He left the Republicans because his campaign
failed to achieve any kind of traction with the American voters.

I always enjoyed watching Pat Buchanan on TV. I even appeared once
on his show. I thought he was gregarious, combative, and enter-
taining. I knew his political position was far to the right, but until he
published his public embrace of Adolf Hitler, I didn't realize how
dangerous his views are on a broad range of subjects.

In September I read a review of Buchanan's book and couldn't believe my eyes. He actually said the Western allies were wrong to stop Hitler. He argued that we should have let Hitler take all the territories to his east—Poland, Hungary, Czechoslovakia, and parts of the Soviet Union. What of the systematic annihilation of Jews, Catholics, and Gypsies in those countries? You don't have to be a genius to know that we were next, that once Hitler seized control of the countries to his east he would focus on world domination. Several historians have pointed out already that Hitler acknowledged plans to attack America as early as 1928. He also worked to acquire islands off Spain and Portugal as ports for super battleships that would attack our navy. He ordered the building of the Amerika Bomber, which could drop five-ton bombs on New York City and return to Europe without refueling. He didn't name it that because he admired us.

On top of everything else, Hitler declared war on the United States. He didn't want us to get the jump on him. He would have felt unmanly.

I sent an assistant out to get the book. A more complete reading confirmed the review I had read.

Pat Buchanan was actually preaching the same policy of appeasement that had failed for Neville Chamberlain at Munich. If we used Buchanan's theory on Hitler as a foreign-policy strategy, we would have appeased every world dictator with a screw loose and we'd have a brainwashed population ready to go postal on command. We'd be in trouble all over the globe. And the iron curtain would still be standing.

I learned that Buchanan was appearing on *Face the Nation* Sunday morning, September 19. I called and dictated a statement critical of Buchanan on Hitler and had it faxed to the show.

I was surprised by the reaction of the New York and national media after I criticized Buchanan's outlandish views. I was splashed across the headlines as the first public figure to criticize the conservative columnist. Beyond me, Buchanan's views were met with deafening silence from the professional politicians. The Anti-Defamation League of B'nai B'rith had to call on John McCain, Elizabeth Dole, Steve Forbes, George W. Bush, and several lesser-known candidates to ask them to respond to Buchanan's remarks. It took three days for them to react. This underscores the central problem with contemporary politicians. They are so concerned with winning votes that they cannot even find it in themselves to immediately denounce a man who winks at barbarism. Why was I, a nonpolitician, the first to challenge Buchanan's outrageous views publicly? I was honored when Abe Foxman of the Anti-Defamation League of B'nai B'rith, one of the most respected Jewish leaders in the country, called to commend me.

After I contacted *Face the Nation,* Buchanan fired back accusing me of "ignorance." Buchanan, who believes himself an expert, has also called Hitler "a political organizer of the first rank." He has said, ". . . Hitler's success was not based on his extraordinary gifts alone. His genius was an intuitive sense of the mushiness, the character flaws, the weakness masquerading as morality that was in the hearts of the statesmen who stood in his path." Buchanan is a fan. My point of view represents what I think the whole world understands—that Hitler was a madman and a murderer of millions.

Buchanan's views on Hitler convinced me to find out more about his record, and the more I read the more outraged I became.

Buchanan has a long history of defending Nazi war criminals and actually argued that the death camps at Treblinka couldn't have executed anyone because the poison gas used was not toxic enough to kill. Buchanan's theory seems to be that Jews took over American foreign policy after the war and lied to us about everything, that Jewish global interests were paramount in American governmental thinking, and that they even outweighed United States security interests. The death camps? "Group fantasies of martyrdom," he called them. Even as serious a commentator as William F. Buckley said, "I find it impossible to defend Pat Buchanan against the charge that what he did and said . . . amounted to anti-Semitism. . . ."

Pat Buchanan has been guilty of many egregious examples of intolerance. He has systematically bashed Blacks, Mexicans, and Gays. In 1983, saying that homosexuals had "declared war on nature," he said that AIDS is nature's "awful retribution." Only three years ago he said that he would not hire Gays in his administration. He believes Gays are "hellbent on Satanism and suicide."

In 1983 he said, "Women are simply not endowed by nature with the same measures of single-minded ambition and the will to succeed in the fiercely competitive world of Western capitalism."

Of the big cities, Buchanan said that "quasi-dictatorial rule" might be the solution: "If the people are corrupt, the more democracy, the worse the government."

He spoke out in favor of apartheid.

Buchanan's extremist views have to be challenged by someone.

A number of circumstances have conspired to conceal the fact that Buchanan is close to the lunatic fringe. His strong showing against George Bush in 1992 seemed to make him a mainstream candidate. But this primary came at a time of extreme economic dislocation and was a direct result of the perception that George Bush could not fathom the difficulties working people were encountering in a cooling economy.

(In a way, the criticism that Bush was out of touch was true. A golf pro I know once told me of a conversation he overheard between President Bush and Treasury Secretary Nick Brady on the back nine one day. Bush asked Brady how the economy was doing and Brady said, "Hell, Mr. President, I spoke to the guys at my club"—meaning his country club—"and they're all doing great."

George Bush was one of the most decent, honorable, and honest men ever elected president, but he failed to comprehend that he was in the bubble created by the American presidency and simply lost touch with what the American people were thinking and feeling.)

In 1996 Buchanan won the New Hampshire primary because of the inherent weakness of the Dole candidacy and because Steve Forbes's relentless pounding on Dole created an opening for Buchanan.

It is interesting that in both 1992 and 1996, Buchanan's candidacy began unraveling immediately after his New Hampshire successes as voters began to focus on his outlandish opinions.

I think the problem is that for twenty-five years Pat Buchanan has been a columnist required to churn out unconventional and newsworthy views on a weekly basis. Only late in his life did he decide to shift to electoral politics and seek the presidency. Simply put, Pat Buchanan has written too many inflammatory, outrageous, and controversial things to ever be elected president.

Buchanan's designs on the Reform Party nomination, and particularly his designs on the $12.6 million that the federal government will provide for the general-election campaign of the Reform Party nominee, clearly upset my friend Governor Ventura.

Although Jesse and Buchanan may have some economic views in common, Buchanan's rigid, right-wing position on social issues would be anathema to many younger voters and could scare them away from ever considering the Reform Party.

Another Schroth poll of Reform Party voters in October showed me in a statistical dead heat with Pat Buchanan and my numbers were coming up. Clearly I could defeat Buchanan in a campaign for the Reform Party presidential nomination. If I ran for the nomination I would refuse federal matching funds. If I were nominated I would accept federal funds. I would refuse to grovel for campaign cash from any special interest. I would spend from my own funds whatever it took to win.

(I recall a quote from President John F. Kennedy when asked how much his father, Ambassador Joseph P. Kennedy, intended to spend to elect his son in 1960. "Whatever it takes and not a penny more," said JFK.)

I think Buchanan got the message that I'm a serious contender, because a few days later, appearing on CNN's *Late Edition with Wolf Blitzer*, Buchanan seemed to be in retreat from the Reform Party, saying he didn't think he could win.

My star, however, seemed to be rising. In early October I announced formation of a committee to explore a run for the presidency. At that time I announced that my first choice for vice president would be Oprah Winfrey. Again the political elites chortled—Oprah Winfrey! They just don't understand how many Americans respect and admire Oprah for her intelligence and caring. She has provided inspiration for millions of women to improve their lives, go back to school, learn to read, and take responsibility for themselves. If I can't get Oprah, I'd like someone like her.

I have been surprised by the way the national media has handled the possibility of a Trump candidacy. Some people find it outlandish that someone outside of the world of professional politics could seek the American presidency. There is much gnashing of teeth among the pundits about the fact that we have become a celebrity culture in which businessmen, movie stars, athletes, and newscasters can be considered for public office. Yes, celebrity *may* get you to the table of American politics. Sure it helps when 97 percent of the people know who you are. But after that, voters are looking for accomplishments and qualifications. I run a billion-dollar corporation. I have created thousands of well-paying jobs. I make decisions every day that affect the livelihoods of thousands of people. I have to keep a constant eye on the bottom line to make sure that my company is efficient and profitable. Perhaps it's time that America was run this way.

Unlike candidates from the two major parties, my candidacy would not represent an exercise in career advancement. I am not a political pro trying to top off his resumé. I am considering a run only because I am convinced that the major parties have lost their way.

The Republicans, especially those in Congress, are captives of their right wing. The Democrats are captives of their left wing. I don't hear anyone speaking for the working men and women in the center. There is very little contact between the concerns and interests of ordinary people and the agendas of politicians. It was my observation of this gap between Americans and their "leaders" that led me to leave the Republican Party and join the Reform Party. The Reform Party carries a lot less baggage than the major parties. It has an opportunity to truly overhaul our political system in service of the American Dream.

Do I need to be president to feel good about myself? I feel pretty good right now. People say I do things because I have a big ego. I've never met a person who's successful who didn't have an ego. There's nothing wrong with it. I get teased for putting the Trump name on my buildings and casinos. Mostly it's a marketing strategy; Trump buildings get higher rents. A similar building across the street cannot command the rent a Trump building can because in my business Trump means quality. I've been teased about whether I'd like to see the name Trump on the White House. I pledge I would not rename the White House. I would only want my name on the desk in the Oval Office.

I would bring a different approach to the presidency. I am convinced that the challenges we will soon face will require a president who is not fixated on popularity polls and reelection. I would enter office with the understanding that four years hence I would be back in New York doing the job I love.

What are those challenges? I agree with many respected economists that the economy may take a dramatic downturn in the near future. Having prevailed over a severe (and largely government-created) setback in my own industry, I know the tough decisions a chief executive has to make to return to prosperity. There are no easy roads back, and poll-watching pols who insist otherwise and govern accordingly will only prolong the problem.

Americans can also be assured that I would never support what has to be one of the craziest ideas in the history of U.S. politics: allowing the government to invest Social Security retirement funds in the stock market. Not only would a market downturn spell disaster

273

for millions of retirees, but the process by which government would choose stocks would also be entirely political, making lobbyists and other political hacks the new masters of the universe.

Our international adversaries would also note a significant change. North Korea would suddenly discover that its worthless promises of civilized behavior would cut no ice. I would let Pyongyang know in no uncertain terms that it can either get out of the nuclear arms race or expect a rebuke similar to the one Ronald Reagan delivered to Moammar Ghadhafi in 1986.

I have no illusions. A Trump candidacy would do best in an economic downturn, when American voters would likely turn to a can-do businessman prepared to make the tough decisions. No one can tell what the economy will be like in 2000, but it will impact my decision.

Some people think it would be a bad idea to have a president who has been in the casino gaming business. But the casino business is the most tightly regulated business in America. The New Jersey Casino Control Commission rigorously investigates everyone seeking to hold a casino license, to ensure their honesty, integrity, financial stability, and to guarantee that they have no links, however tenuous, to organized crime. One thing you can say about Trump, as the holder of a casino gaming license, is that I'm 100 percent clean—something you can't say with certainty about our current group of presidential candidates.

Just the same, politics and gambling don't mix. My gaming company in Atlantic City has new records for operating cash flow. I have turned down numerous generous offers to buy out my interest in Trump Hotels and Casino Resorts. If I decide to run for president I'd be prepared to divest myself of my gaming industry holdings or put them in a blind trust.

I don't think anybody is going to accuse me of tiptoeing through the issues or tap-dancing around them either. Who else in public life has called for the extradition and trial of Fidel Castro, or for a preemptive strike on North Korea? I think I've also made a good case for shaking up things at home, whether in calling for real choice in education, healthcare, retirement accounts, or in giving America's entrepreneurs the best shot possible at success.

I've also put forward my plan for America to begin the next century debt free. By imposing a one-time 14.25 percent net-worth tax on the wealthiest members of our society we can raise $5.7 billion in new taxes, pay off the national debt entirely, and save $200 billion in interest annually. Then we can use the money saved to cut taxes on the middle class by $1 trillion over ten years, repeal the inheritance tax and still have $3 trillion over the next thirty years to bolster the Social Security Trust Fund.

My plan will only affect the top 1 percent of Americans. The net result for the other 99 percent will be a sharp drop in personal income tax rates. By imposing a one-time 14.25 percent net-worth tax on the richest individuals and trusts, we can put America on a sound financial footing for the next century.

My plan will personally cost me hundreds of millions of dollars, but it would be worth it.

I am convinced that as more and more Americans learn of my plan and more people understand it, the more popular it will become. Is that a good reason to run for president? We will see.

Some will call my propositions radical, but I beg to differ. The fact is, my positions are conservative—in the traditional sense. They are built on traditional American values, especially the right of the individual to determine his or her fate. Our history teaches that progress begins with the individual. When you tie the hands of the individual, you have slipped a noose around the neck of the American Dream.

Nor can anyone accuse me of sugarcoating the challenges we face. Eearly readers of this manuscript thought my warnings about chemical and biological threats were overstated. Then we learned that the government is placing sensors around New York to detect attack. But my other hope—that established public figures would bring this discussion to center stage—is still largely unrealized. Perhaps this book will help us to start that discussion.

I truly believe Americans want straight talk on these issues, yet there is precious little straight talk coming from our political and media rainmakers. The result couldn't be clearer: We are suffering a leadership crisis. I use the word *crisis* because we face huge challenges and threats, yet our leadership, for the most part, is dodging the hard issues, from Medicare to the bioterrorism threat to the crisis in public education.

So what do we do? We don't wring our hands. Instead we do what Americans have always done. We flush the deadwood. We field a new team. The question is not "can we overcome this crisis in leadership?" It is, instead, "where do we find the new generation of America's leaders?"

★　　　★　　　★

I would center my presidency on three principles: one term, two-fisted policies, and no excuses. For voters it would be a business approach, and the best one available in the presidential marketplace. I'd lead by example. And what I could also bring to the presidency is a new spirit, a great spirit that we haven't had in this country for a long time—the kind of spirit that built the American Dream.

Roll Call

ONE OF THE THEMES OF this book has been my belief that we ought to marshal the smartest, most capable, most successful people in America and enlist their ideas and their energy in building the America We Deserve. Where will we find the leaders? I've already talked about my admiration for Governor Ventura and Jack Welch.

Another, as I also mentioned, is Oprah Winfrey. She is enormously successful in an incredibly competitive field. Not only has she overcome huge obstacles to reach the very top, but she's also gone well beyond ordinary celebrity status as an entertainer to become a major cultural influence on our times and a remarkably successful businesswoman. Oprah never forgets what is important, and she never stops encouraging Americans to reach for the stars.

I'm not going to list all the good things Oprah has done to make this country better, but one does stand out in my mind, especially since I've been thinking about education issues for this book. Oprah has inspired millions of young women to get an education and improve their lives. And how many television personalities make such an issue of getting members of their audience to read? Her viewers have certainly responded, which has made Oprah a literary king-maker and queenmaker. Authors featured by her book club suddenly find themselves on the bestsellers list.

There are many, many Americans who are fully dedicated to helping fellow citizens improve their minds. God bless all of them. And I think all of them will agree that Oprah is on the side of the angels, and may even be an angel herself. Oprah exemplifies the leadership I'm interested in—she doesn't strike poses. Instead she poses striking questions: Are you doing your best? If not, why not?

Then there's my good friend Bob Torricelli, the brilliant senator from New Jersey. He's a first-rate public figure. He knows Castro is a dictatorial bum and he has held a tough line on the embargo issue. Bob knows, as I know, that any investment in Cuba supports Castro's oppressive rule. We'll wait until he's gone. Next year in Havana? Let's hope so.

The Torch also knows that tax cuts work economic wonders. His advocacy of a cut, over the objections of the Democratic Senate leadership, took guts. That brings us to Bob's big problem, at least as far as a lot of Washington types are concerned. He's independent. That scares Beltway types, who believe in the party line and nothing else. They are like lemmings, and when they head for the deep water they'll try to take the rest of us down with them. Independent thinkers like Bob Torricelli are the kinds of leaders that will stand between us and disaster in a tight time. I am truly honored to have him as a close friend.

People are sometimes nervous about meeting Muhammad Ali. For such a great leader and powerful athlete to be incapacitated at such an early age seems shocking. But Muhammad has stood up to his illness with incredible poise. He remains as great an inspiration as he ever was: proud, brash, filled with integrity, a graceful man of principle. No one ever made social change seem as much fun as did Ali. He is still a good citizen and a good father. And on the spiritual level, I believe, he still floats like a butterfly and stings like a bee. It is a joy to see him. And his mere presence—as at the Olympics in Atlanta— would dignify any meeting.

Another person I'd call on has a familiar name: Hoffa. That's Jim Hoffa, the new president of the International Brotherhood of Teamsters. He has all of his old man's good qualities—toughness, fairness, and an unbelievable talent for perseverance—with none of the bad. Before he moved to the top of the union line he was a street-smart labor lawyer. His knees don't jerk, and if anyone knows how to bring the Teamsters back to their rightful place at the table, Jim is that man.

Some of my conservative friends are frowning. Is Trump a union man? Let me tell you this: Unions still have a place in American society. In fact, with the globalization craze in full heat, unions are about the only political force reminding us to remember the American working family. Does that make me an America First-er? When it comes to protecting the jobs of American families, I'll gladly step to the front of that line. And this is no cheap stance on my part. I've had innumerable requests to do business overseas. Before I make any decision, I always check to see how it will impact American wage earners. This has cost me plenty, but when I see American companies put profit before patriotism, it makes me ill.

Florida Governor Jeb Bush is a good man. I've held fundraisers for him. He's exactly the kind of political leader this country needs now and will very much need in the future. He, too, knows how to hang in there. His first shot at Florida's governorship didn't work out, but he didn't give up. He was campaigning the day after his loss. He won the next race in a landslide. He's bright, tough, and principled. I like the Bush family very much. I believe we could get another president from the Bushes. He may be the one.

I'm also very positive about Susan Molinari. She has the same qualities of brightness, toughness, and principle. I know she's off the political stage right now, but I'm also convinced that when the nation needs her she'll step back onto the scene.

Arlen Specter is another person I respect. He's a tough guy who has also refused to bow to defeat. He has had plenty of opportunities to be a quitter. He ran for mayor of Philadelphia and lost. Then he lost his race for the governorship of Pennsylvania. A Senate race ended the same way. Three strikes, but he definitely was not out. In 1980 he won his first Senate race, and has won two subsequent races, both of them tough.

I like Arlen for a lot of reasons, especially because he's a tough, no-nonsense, law-and-order guy. We really need to keep guys like him around, because we're seeing a backlash against strong anticrime policies. Crime rates are down. Public confidence is up. And the criminal lobby is fighting back. Guys like Arlen will help us keep the gains we've made.

Which brings me to my good friend Rudy Giuliani—a genuine national hero. He has shown the nation how to reduce crime by making New York safer than it's been for decades. A lot of that can be attributed to Giuliani's no-nonsense policies. Rudy is also a traditional conservative, at least in the sense that I think of the word. He has built his policies on the traditional value of personal responsibility.

Rudy has also reminded us that healthy societies don't let the small stuff slide, because small problems add up to big problems. By enforcing the laws on the books that his predecessors dismissed as "trivial," he has changed the tone and tenor of New York. The city hasn't felt this good for a long, long time. But this doesn't rub everyone the right way. The Pure and Precious members of the photo-op morality club have been hounding Rudy. I stand with him, as I'm sure most Americans do. I'm looking forward to supporting him in his bid for the U.S. Senate against a certain lady named Hillary. I'm 100 percent for Rudy Giuliani but Hillary Clinton is definitely smart and resilient. She was very nice to my sons, Donny and Eric, when she visited New York.

(The whole Clinton story became a tragedy. Bill Clinton could have gone down as a very good president. Instead he goes down as a guy they tried to impeach. Now he can't even get into a golf club in Westchester. But he can join my golf club—I'd be proud to have him. I'm developing a spectacular new country club five minutes from his new home.

And speaking of his new home, in all candor, he really overpaid. He really got ripped off on the house. If I had represented him in buying the house I could have saved them about $600,000.)

Equal to Rudy, at least in my book, is George Pataki, the governor of New York, the most underrated guy in American politics. This guy, after all, felled the great Mario Cuomo, once a political giant—and in some minds one of the nation's biggest windbags. George took down Mario and transformed New York State into a business-friendly environment. He cut taxes. He restored the death penalty. I'm looking for him on one end of the Republican ticket in 2000 or the other end in 2004.

The best political leaders aren't always politicians. Ross Perot has never gotten the credit he deserves for making America a better place. No, he didn't get elected president, but he never expected to—so let's drop all the nonsense that Ross was on a free-spending ego trip. He spent his own money to put some very important public policy ideas in play, and if you look around you'll see that the agenda he ran on in 1992 and 1996 has been adopted by both parties and, in some of its particulars, enacted into law.

The balanced budget he championed is now a reality. He wasn't the first to advocate this, but he kept the idea alive. Campaign finance reform, one of Ross's central issues, is now gaining strength in Congress. People made fun of Ross's speaking style but he almost always said the right things. And you could depend on Perot to speak to the heart of an issue. He put substance ahead of style, and we are much richer for it.

If I could pick the next cabinet I'd look to Jack Welch, of General Electric, for secretary of the treasury. Welch, as I said, is a guy who is brilliant, who understands American business inside and out in a profound way, and who is also a great communicator. He's the top guy in his field. A guy like Welch wouldn't join the government unless something in national politics changes. But he's exactly the type of person a Trump administration would bring to Washington.

You want to meet a really tough guy? I have to mention General Alexander Lebed, who came to my office a few years ago to try to convince me to develop real estate and build a casino in his native Russia. I expect him to become the most important man in Russia's future. He will have a big impact on us as well. As the political system collapses in his country, look for this hard-boiled character to grab power for one purpose: to save Russia from backsliding into communism.

The general is definitely up to the job. He's steely-eyed, cagey, outspoken, and resourceful. I'm sure no one down in the State Department has him on their list of potential presidents, but when Yeltsin falls, I'm looking for the general to step up to the plate.

Politics can be a pretty tough and jaded game, and there are precious few players who radiate the optimism and sense of possibility that must remain at the heart of our system. One who does is Oklahoma congressman J. C. Watts. I admire J. C. for his passion and principle. As an African American Republican a lot of critical eyes are on him, and he's used to being dismissed by those who think they know how African American politicians are supposed to vote. Yet he sticks to his beliefs. He's also a national treasure as a role model for our young people. While we should maintain a healthy skepticism toward public figures, knee-jerk skepticism and cynicism jeopardize the very faith on which our system is built. J. C. is a very substantial check on that tendency.

Now that I've broached the subject of cynicism and skepticism, I need to point out that a few people wouldn't make my list. They are the antithesis of the kind of leaders we need in Millennium Three.

On top of that list is Bill Bradley, whose bumbling I discussed in detail in my chapter on economics. I continue to be astounded that people swoon at this guy's feet. He's as phony as a twenty-dollar Rolex. The fact that Bradley is running for president as a Washington outsider is one of the biggest jokes in politics. He is a deep insider, and has unleashed disastrous policies that cost thousands of people their jobs during what some people still call his "distinguished" service as a senator.

Many analysts insist that Bradley is the perfect guy to rescue the Democratic Party from the Clinton taint. That's ridiculous. Al Gore is a much more formidable intellect and public servant than Bradley. I remember when he bested Ross Perot in their famous debate, and I can assure you that I disagree strongly with some of Gore's political positions. But he is also vastly underrated, and I believe he'll send Bradley back to Jersey with his well-worn tail between his legs.

Here's another presidential joke: Lowell Weicker. I read where this former Connecticut senator and governor is considering a presidential run in 2000 as an Independent. I'm wondering: Independent of what? Has he finally gained independence from his one-time status as one of Washington's premier windbags and as, quite frankly, a man capable of telling colossal lies to voters? This is the guy who promised the people of Connecticut that if elected governor he wouldn't support a state income tax—and then turned around and put one through the legislature and signed it into law.

If Weicker does decide to run, maybe he should join forces with New York congressman Jerry Nadler, one of the most egregious hacks in contemporary politics. This guy wanted to put a railroad yard on the same property where I wanted to build a park and create the best middle-income housing in New York. I think Nadler believes something is missing when he looks at a skyline and doesn't see a forest of belching smokestacks. He and Weicker would fit well together because they are politicians of the past. There is definitely no room for them, or politicians like them, in America's future.

Earlier this year Senator Bob Smith of New Hampshire dropped out of the Republican presidential contest and attacked the party "for deserting conservative principles." Smith's real problem was that his candidacy was attracting no votes. The good senator, who was reelected to his last term in the Senate by a hair, knew he would be defeated if he ran again. Rather than face up to the fact that he and his views were most unattractive to Republican voters, he decided that it was the party's fault for not wanting him. This is the kind of depraved thinking that goes on among the professional politicians in Washington. In the television age, Bob Smith is about the least attractive candidate I can imagine—inarticulate, unqualified, and, according to several members I know, about the dumbest guy in the U.S. Senate.

When my sister Maryanne Barry Trump, one of the brightest and most capable people on the federal bench, appeared before the Senate Judiciary Committee in a hearing on her elevation to a federal judgeship in the Third Circuit Court, Smith insisted on asking her views on abortion. She patiently explained to the good senator that her personal views on the issue were meaningless; a federal judge's job is to uphold the law as it is written, not to interpret from the bench based on his or her personal views. Maybe if my sister had spoken more slowly he would have understood her.

★ ★ ★

I see huge challenges before us. But I also see a nation that has survived everything fate has thrown at it and come out better every time.

I know that when these challenges come, we will come together as a people, and we will find the leaders we need. Where? I don't know exactly. Maybe on a farm in the Midwest, on a California hilltop, or in a small Virginia town. Maybe our next great leader—one with the cunning of Franklin Roosevelt, the guts of Harry Truman, the resilience of Richard Nixon, and the optimism of Ronald Reagan—is walking down Fifth Avenue right now, straight through the heart of this land of dreamers and shakers—this land that I love.

ABOUT THE AUTHOR

DONALD J. TRUMP is president and chief executive officer of the Trump Organization. A billionaire developer, he has transformed the landscape of Manhattan and been active in the Atlantic City hotel/casino industry. His three books, *Trump: The Art of the Deal, Trump: Surviving at the Top,* and *Trump: The Art of the Comeback,* have all been best sellers. He has four children and lives in New York City.

DAVE SHIFLETT has served as an editor and columnist at the *Denver Rocky Mountain News.* His writing has appeared in the *Weekly Standard,* the *Wall Street Journal, Reader's Digest,* and other journals. He lives in Midlothian, Virginia, with his wife, Susan, and two sons.